BAGS OF (

Every Womar

ABOUT THE AUTHORS

Lorna Hogg is single, and a Dublin based journalist and broadcaster. For the past twenty years she has written for a variety of Irish and British newspapers and magazines on topics ranging from finance and royalty to gardening and alternative health.

Technophobic and entirely undomesticated, she has raised an innate lack of interest in housework to an art form. She was inspired to write this book by the number of women she has met, well-known and as yet undiscovered, who have re-invented themselves. She herself has succeeded at this, re-incarnating through student, to company director, farm manager and journalist.

Like Sally, Lorna believes that a woman can have a great life at any age, whether single, semi-attached or entirely detached.

Sally Moon was born in the late 30s at a time when the limit of many women's ambition was marriage. Expensively, but sketchily educated she went on to marry and divorce twice, discovering after the end of each that the only investment she had made in the relationships were emotional ones.

Finding herself alone in her twenties was relatively painless, however, the same could not be said when she found herself single again, but this time in her 50s.

Now she lives quietly in the country, playing at training gundogs, doing a bit of public speaking and entertaining her sons and grandchildren. In fact back where she started, but with many hitherto unknown talents.

Lorna and Sally can be contacted at
oldbagsclub@hotmail.com

BAGS OF OPPORTUNITY

Every Woman's Guide to Re-Invention

Lorna Hogg

and

Sally Moon

ASHFIELD
Press

This book was typeset by Artwerk Limited for

Ashfield Press,
8 Priory Hall, Stillorgan,
Co. Dublin,
Ireland.

Email: ashfieldpress@eircom.net
Website: www.blackhallpublishing.com

A catalogue record for this book is available from the British
Library

ISBN: 1 901658 24 4

Printed in Ireland by
ColourBooks Ltd

CONTENTS

INTRODUCTION:
BY SALLY MOON

How I wish this book had been around when I first found myself alone, penniless, without training and worst of all (as I saw it then) middle aged. Having run up countless blind alleyways, what I needed was a few well sign-posted directions. I had spent so many hours fulminating and stamping around in a rage that I had virtually alienated most of my friends. I lost what little money I had in useless enterprises. Enterprises which to the streetwise were patently not the "get rich quick" they purported to be. I had allowed suspicion and intolerance to get the better of me. Instead of taking a gentle reasoning tone, I used a confrontational abrasive method. The problems out there seemed insurmountable, there were so many, I should have taken them slowly, one at a time. Now I know it was ignorance and fear of the unknown which drove me to ever more reckless actions.

This book is a must for those contemplating stepping into that wilderness alone, and for those who find themselves there through no fault of their own. Had I a manual, which clearly outlined all the possibilities and certainties of life out here, I might have taken a calmer and more rational attitude to the dilemma I found myself in. All the books that dealt with spiritual and personal therapy were not for me. I thought I had a good idea of who I was...*viz.* a trusting person, but not a fool. What I needed was clear unambiguous information, not physco babble that simply delayed the evil hour of fending for myself. Victim I was not, a vile pejorative to which I react with fury. I have met so many women who paint themselves into the picture of "victim" under the false allusion that they will attract sympathy. Nevertheless, there were times when it was quite hard to hang onto the fact that you still have a voice and will of your own – such is the power that those who have money exert over those of us who have little. That fact alone can diminish your self-respect faster than anything else. If I remember my solicitor for anything other than his swingeing bills, it is for his proclamation as he stood full bellied and complacent, saying "remember Sally, cash is power". How right he was!

For many years I had been aware that this leaky vessel, euphemistically called a marriage, was heading slowly but irrevocably onto the rocks. But as time went on I resolutely turned my head away from all its failings and attempted to count my blessings. I had a roof over my head, a car to drive, none of the usual household bills to pay, a conventional social life ... and as I grew older and vaguely aware, of societies' disinterest in the middle aged, I counted those blessings ever faster. There was a time when I did it so well that complacency, the oldest enemy of marriage, sat happily on my shoulder.

However, the time came when the decision was no longer mine. Our lovely house, although in our joint names, was sold without consultation and we moved to a large rented ruin, miles from all my friends and family. So deeply was the patriarchal indoctrination ingrained within my soul that it never occurred to me to question why we did not simply buy a smaller house if money was the root of the trouble. I had been taught to trust the leader and, as that had always been a man in my life, so it continued. Discussing anything other than immediate mundane domestic finances was met with sharp rebuttals. We had only bought a short lease on the ruin, thankfully in our joint names, a fact I took for granted at the time, but for which I was to be eternally grateful eventually. The sale released quite a substantial amount of capital, which was swiftly spirited out of the country. Although I was dimly aware of the fact, as usual I did not question it. Again patriarchy won the day.

The final demise of our marriage was as common as the death of so many other partnerships, but my eventual reaction to it was a violent demonstration for him alone I thought, not the outside world. I was not the gullible victim I appeared to be. In hindsight I am appalled that I could have done anything so incriminating, so designed to prejudice my case and a fair settlement. After years of living in the twilight of married ignorance, all I was aware of was that "things" were being managed for me yet again. Short breaks of lucidity in the clouds of incomprehension only added to my frustration. I learnt you need the support and love of friends, not their well-meaning bits of misinformation, which simply served to fuel the ever-growing inferno of rage and sense of impotence. I will admit that I finally gave in to jealousy, a perfectly normal emotion in the circumstances, but one that I had not been guilty of within the marriage. Jealousy, or rather the hold it had of me, is a terrifying condition. I think it was Stendahl who said, "Jealousy is like being chained to a madman". In other words its victim is dragged hither and thither without purpose or reason – their actions at times reckless, dangerous and even life threatening.

Having been divorced once before, I thought I had learnt not to make the same mistakes again. Then I had allowed the full force of male dominance to manipulate the eventual outcome of that disintegration to profit only them. Letters flying between expensive London solicitors, with highly edited contributions from us the litigants, only served to build up bitter incriminations in what had been a fairly reasonable relationship. The final outcome was to be to the children's disadvantage and the triumph of male pride. This must not be allowed to happen again and to that end I tried to keep the legal intervention to the minimum and the lines of communications with him at least civil. We used a modified form of mediation, which at least reduced the occurrence of those inflammatory letters. My requests were reasonable – such was my desire to stay on friendly terms with this man to whom I had been married for 25 years and who was the father of my sons, and with whom I had had some good times. I wanted that rare thing, a friendly divorce ... a contradiction if ever I heard one. I made it easy for him. I made it so easy in fact that he assumed I was handling the break-up well, that I was not lonely and frightened, that I was happy to watch on the sidelines the easy continuation of his life, with a new set of friends, a lover and a social life. He was in demand, there was always a place at the dinner table for him, and in fact he was a welcome new face. Slowly the full realisation of just what life after divorce was going to be like for me, the mature woman, began to sink in.

First time round in my twenties, moving on was a piece of cake. Now the feeling was of being of a lower species, relegated to a life of kitchen suppers with other divorced women, as though your presence is a disease, which is contagious to other happy couples. I used to take a black sort of comfort that perhaps I was seen as a threat to other women's husbands. In fact I remember one woman saying "next time John is away you must come round and have a meal". Was I going to bore John, or steal John? Now I don't care, but then I minded dreadfully. John was an amusing, intelligent man whose company I had always enjoyed. Slowly the options were being cut down for me, and there was nothing I could do about it. Striking out on one's own takes a hell of a lot of courage when the break is still raw, not forgetting that your ability to get out and about is severely curtailed by lack of funds. The friends you had when you were a couple drop away, you are the frightening reality of fiscal and sexual powerlessness. Your sleep pattern changes as you wake at two o'clock in the morning, endlessly and irrationally going over the minutiae of your jealousy, your finances, your despair. Walking round the house eases the hurt, but does not help to separate the problems into their component parts; they amalgamate into one huge intolerable weight. I honestly think that had anyone seen me in that semi-manic state I might well have been locked up in the mad wing along with Mrs. Rochester.

Then you crack – and you have to, otherwise the nightmare continues and the condition becomes chronic, sealing your fate as a bitter woman, that most despised of all creatures.

My crack – or rather explosion took the form of the sort of impetuous action which was very much in keeping with my nature. It is *not* the way for everyone. Of course in the middle of the silly season it was manna from the gods for the press. For me it was just therapy. The desecration of a beautiful car, the one arm sleeve amputation of tens of expensive suits and the final act, one of philanthropy at least, the wine distribution to the worthy people of the village, was pure release. Had I known another less risky route then I would have taken it.

That was an end, it was all I wanted. I knew where the soft underbelly was and I had made good use of that knowledge. I was recognised once again, or so I thought. Where to go from there? I had no idea, the scenario was as it had been and materially I was no better off. In fact I was in a worse position. All financial help was cut off. Although I had stopped the divorce proceeding, he then took the initiative and I was forced back into the hands of far more expensive and time-consuming lawyers. This was when fate stepped in, and thanks to the extraordinary interest of the press I was given an opportunity (all be it unconventional) to find in myself strength, a voice and above all humour. I got all the attention even the most self-seeking person could have wished for. I travelled to America, to Europe, to Ireland and appeared on television. I spoke on radio to Australia, New Zealand, Japan and Canada. I sat on every chat show you could name. It seems I had struck just the right chord with so many women of my age – I was their surrogate avenger. Work in journalism and television came flooding in, the sort of breaks that many far more deserving people than I would have given their eye teeth for. However you might just as well have given rubies to a baby such was my inability to appreciate their true worth.

It was wonderful while it lasted, but there was no getting round the fact that I had to do up "cold turkey" and that was when the real learning game began. That was when I learnt that although I had a better idea of where to go for sensible help I still had no experience of the merciless world of money. A world when even within the family (where rules are unspoken and jurisdiction unenforceable), as a single woman you are not only seen as fair game but set up for exploitation. Like some elderly ingénue I emerged into a world where youth with its bravery born of ignorance has reason to be forgiven its mistakes, but you with your wrinkles are deemed to know better. No holds are barred and you have to watch your back.

As the press interest has died I have been left with the bare bones of real strength and a courage I never imagined I possessed. I have new good friends not just social acquaintances. I move in a different social circle. I have found talents I never knew I had. I have a new material shrewdness (not that attractive, but a necessary evil). I had to find the courage to face the future knowing that there is no pension and that even the basic state pension has not been contributed to. I will always be a muddler, but only because professionals have put the financial infrastructure in place. Professionals I have chosen, whom I like and trust, and keep me informed and up to date.

As I intimated earlier, it is my belief that the money thing has got to be tackled before moving onto the emotional repair work. Money oils everything, but money, which you control, is top grade oil. Many women, myself included, have a huge urge to replace the old partner with a new model. Although one would never overtly admit it, there is the need to prove that one is still sexually desirable. Heaven forbid that one could be so crude or basic! I feel in hindsight that attaching all ones hopes of a swift repatriation into the world of couples and its perceived security is foolish. That is not moving on, it is simply retreading the same stale ground. You need to grow...I hate this kind of "speak", it is not in my normal vocabulary. However by "grow" I mean have a damn good look at your old values, acknowledge the basic virtues but be strong enough to chuck out those old dated attitudes. You may well be socialising with people from a world you may not recognise and probably did not know existed. People you have had no need to cultivate in the past may suddenly present new challenges and interests. Safe within relationships one can be either too frightened or lazy to try new stamping grounds. Now however you have to change. I remember waking up one morning and realising I had three men on the boil so to speak, two married bastards and an "also ran". I felt tired, used and disgusted with myself. I suppose I had proved something, but in hindsight it seems of little value. There is a type of man, usually married, who can sense a vulnerable woman from a mile away. A woman who has so little self esteem that she measures her worth in direct relation to her sexual power. These men circle round like vultures waiting for the opportune moment to lap down and press their dubious charms on their weak victim. She, poor self-deluded creature, will latch onto him like a drowning man, thereby inflating his already falsely grounded ego. I feel they should be seen for what they are, used if you wish and then discarded. It may be a simplistic form of retaliation when two wrongs do not make a right, but if that is what it takes to get on with the healing therapy, then so be it. It is definitely not a philosophy for life however.

I have set my life up with the expectation that I may well live unmarried for the rest of my days, whilst keeping the antennae gently waving. I do things on my own, and while it is pleasurable to share with a friend, you are aware and appreciate people and things around you on a much deeper level if you do it alone. I go to restaurants on my own; I've been to a ball on my own; I go on holiday on my own, although I am too scared to go abroad on my own I will admit, but I will in due time. I've discovered B&Bs, which are the most wonderful way to meet people. I do not go to pubs on my own, because I do not want to. I can be unconventional and I dress in the way I like. I am an individual not an extension. Some call me formidable. Women with husbands very rarely tackle me, they set their husbands on me, a situation I find highly amusing. Do *not* get yourself in a state about men, and unless you can take dating agencies for what they are, places to meet people, take them with a pinch of salt. Don't worry, they are out there, but believe me not one is Prince Charming...however some are quite nice frogs!

Finally I sometimes wonder just what sort of life it is I am aiming for, now that I have relatively more control. Happiness is so short lived and works best in short bursts. Perhaps it is contentment, not to be mistaken for that impostor complacency. Society is changing even for us more mature women. A woman on her own is seen as an interesting aware creature, not the sad flotsam of a broken relationship.

IT CAN BE DONE

CHAPTER ONE:
ACCEPTANCE

So you're on you own now. It may be from choice, necessity or force of circumstances. You may like the situation, or you may not. You may be feeling nervous and scared, or you may be feeling free and confident. However, whether you *get* to like your situation or not *is* up to you. That's what this book is about. It comes from the experience of many mature women suddenly alone after a lifetime of caring for others. They may have been widowed, divorced, separated, deserted or eventually freed from caring responsibilities, to re-start their lives.

Some were nervous but happy at the prospect. Some were relieved, but frightened. A few were grateful for a second chance. However, many were unhappy, bitter and bewildered at the prospect of change on such a scale. What no one needed was a cheerleading type of book, extolling the benefits of picking yourself up and starting all over again – so we're not providing one. We both hope that it will speak for itself about the options available to women faced with such challenges. And there *are* options. Never in our history has there been a better time to be a mature woman – despite the all-pervading youth culture. In terms of health care, advice, opportunities, education, travel and self-development – we've never had it so good.

Change is an inevitable part of the process, and this frightens most of us. However, part of accepting the reality of a new way of life lies in accepting the necessary changes. And there will be many – perhaps more than you had thought. Changes in finances, lifestyle, relationships, social life and work. Even if you are established in a career, with a social circle of your own, there will be changes. To use a gardening metaphor, a lot of pruning, cutting back and re-seeding will be called for. Some women, however, will have to clear out the deadwood and do some serious weeding before complete re-planting.

It is, of course, a splendid ideal – and like many such ideals will remain so, unless you have the skills necessary to adapt it to your own life circumstances. Many of the fears which women, especially mature women, have about change, are linked to the prospect of being and remaining alone. Alone, in a practical sense of living alone, or feeling emotionally alone and unloved, or even being emotionally alone within a relationship.

Some of these fears are the result of faulty or unrealistic thinking styles. Some are the result of buying into the fantasy of the perfect relationship, and the impossibility of a happy life without one. Some fears are groundless and nonsensical or outmoded. Others are actually reasonable and sensible. It *will* be different when you're faced with one plus none. So let's get the tough bit out of the way at once...

You may have to learn a whole new range of skills – skills that you relied on your partner for. As one woman told us "Even though my husband was a rat, I was very protected and cosseted. It's the minor, even silly things that I'm so shocked by – knowing where to park the car, organising tickets, dealing with officials. And then, of course, there are the major things that left me floundering – coping with builders, mechanics' estimates, and decisions over insurance. I'm not stupid about finance, and I didn't hand everything over to him, but I miss having someone to talk things over with – now I'm responsible for *everything*."

You will have to pay out money for good advice and help. It is possible that as the wife of Joe Bloggs, information, contacts and tips were forthcoming due to your status. Now, you'll have to ensure that not only do you get the best advice, but that you get the best value advice.

Even if the surroundings are the same, the reality is different. If you don't have to leave the home you lovingly created, and you can still look out over the blossoms in spring – can you be sure that you can afford to do so next year?

You may have an urge (sometimes irresistible) to go out and try to re-capture your youth – especially if you feel cheated of it, or that you missed out in some way. Forget about caring relationships – you've been there and bought the tee shirt – what you want are pubs, clubs and girlie nights. If you've been told that you were too prudish, or prissy in your last relationship or marriage, there may be a desire to prove that it just isn't so – to yourself, at any rate.

Some women have the looks, *joie de vivre* and confidence to carry it off and have fun. However, others suffer further indignity and rejection when they try to compete with youth. There is risk involved – to your health and safety, self-esteem, family relationships and inevitable recovery process. Some women may be bitter and vengeful – especially if they've been left for a younger woman, and temporarily abandon their codes about pinching other women's men – of any age. If you're lucky, you can work out this compulsion with a bruised ego and some life experience as the only outcomes. In our non-judgmental world, the only advice given is that the bargain on your side must be silence. Keep your affairs and connections to yourself – don't hurt others, or wreak havoc on the undeserving – it's not their fault.

You could develop depression, perhaps due to isolation, withdrawal from life or emotional exhaustion. Watch out for danger signs – they include changes in eating, sleeping and mood patterns. You may find a disinclination to go out or a lack of interest in seeing old friends, feelings of despair or physical tiredness. Of course, all these signs can also be linked to stress overload, so read up from our list and give yourself some self-help in the early stages when you *can* do so. From time to time we all need to retreat to our caves to lick life's wounds – just make sure you don't set up home permanently in one.

When a household breaks up and family money is split – the parts don't always equal the sum. Rising costs, staffing availability and the economic situation will all now have input into decisions. You may be pressured into selling, or decide that you'd rather not live surrounded by constant reminders that you're clinging to past glories.

This may cause you great heartache and you may feel your dreams are over; not only for an ideal family life, but future successes. You won't be living in the beautiful old mansion in the country, surrounded by family and dogs, with two gleaming cars parked on the gravel. Now he'll have his home (yes, perhaps a country mansion one day, face it) and you'll have your more modest nest. As one woman put it, "in the space of a few months, I moved down the drive, from a terrace round the door to roses round the door – commended residence to condemned cottage!"

To move you on to a new level of depression – realise that you won't be as sought after, as hunted socially or sexually as you were in your twenties. In fact, the cloak of invisibility may socially enshroud you. As Sally says, you change from the dinner party invitation to the lunch drop-in – from the dinner table to the kitchen table. Warning signs include such observations as:

✦   "You must pop round for some supper – Mike's away for a few days."

✦   "Come round one afternoon for a good old chat."

✦   "The brats are back at school – come round for a coffee and catch up."

You have to face the fact that people will see you in a different way, and that your status has changed. One spirited female, determined not to be cast aside after her divorce – and exit from a few charity committees, offered her services to another one. She found herself in a makeshift kitchen, being "really *so* helpful" washing glasses and plates from a filthy, dirty cold tap! That's just the social side, when it comes to relationships, there are some more unpalatable facts to be faced.

You'll have to face the fact that many people won't have the time or interest to invest in getting to know you. This is no reflection on you as a person, merely that in our busy lives, they may have achieved their "quota" of friends.

There will be demotions in status. Your status at the specialist food store may shrink along with your order list. Deliveries may be more difficult to arrange. You may not be requested to join the charity committee this year, and your credit rating may be different.

If your ex-partner has found a replacement, and you all live in the same area, you may have to accustom yourself to the possibility of her sitting in "your" seat at the club, attending that corporate entertainment in your place, and flying Club Class in your stead. Unpalatable and embarrassing though it may be to admit it, some women confess that they often regret the loss of their old role and status as much as their partners.

You'll have to endure the faint astonishment of younger women (all of whom are of course computer literate, financially aware and socially desirable) that you should be in this position in the first place. Even more galling when you are related to some of them.

It will be necessary to grit your teeth at times to endure the unwitting smugness of your remaining married friends. Their blithe assumptions, self-assurance and protected status will induce a range of emotions, ranging from bitterness to anger and regret.

If the reality of life alone, with it's legal, financial and social complexities frightens you, it may be tempting to search for someone else to look after you. You will, however, have to accept that the search will be very difficult. Many introduction agencies find that older men tend to look for younger partners. Even if you do find someone, be aware that assets will probably be reserved for his children. *You* have to take care of you – it's much harder than it used to be to take the calculated step to marry for a pension.

You'll also have to accept the fact that you had a part to play in a relationship which broke down. You can only truly move on when you accept that anger, denial and bitterness merely prolong your misery. No orgies of guilt and self-blame are necessary – and would merely be destructive. But learn from the experience whilst retaining your self-respect. Were you, for instance, too demanding of your partner as a provider? Were you subtly unsupportive about his abilities – sexual, personal, social or professional? Did you help him to achieve his goals and aspirations? Did you deal with any serious problems together, or never really talk about them? Did you meet his needs – or even know what they were? And finally, one of the commonest problems – did he feel deprived of love, or intimacy? Perhaps with some soul-searching you will realise that you were not even married to the right partner in the first place.

You'll also have to be aware that on your own you're vulnerable to a whole range of people whom you will pay to help you – ranging from builders to financial advisors. Don't fall for the patter or the image. Many a woman has come to regret the extension which ate up capital, or lost savings due to advice from the be-suited "city type" with impeccable (and false) credentials.

You'll learn that even with close friends, you'll suffer "slippage" in priorities. In fact, you probably rate beneath the family dog when it comes to attention – but if you're lucky, just above the pet hamster. Accept it – the needs of husbands and children will be paramount, and if Rover needs a vet's visit, your lunch date will be history.

So, after all the horrors, what, if any, are the advantages to being on your own? A variety of women, from a variety of backgrounds, marriages and relationships told us of their particular plusses:

✦ Less cooking.

✦ Less cleaning.

✦ Less pleasing and humouring.

✦ Less required travel, and more travel from choice.

✦ The chance to stay in bed, all day, if desired.

✦ Breakfast in bed, without rows about crumbs.

✦ The chance to see your friends, as often as you want.

✦ No one to make unpleasant comments about your friends, or their influence.

✦ No back seat drivers in the car.

✦ No unwanted sex when you're tired.

✦ No fuss and stress over Christmas and bank holiday weekends.

✦ No required business entertaining.

✦ No more put-downs, snide comments and belittling observations, about weight or hair, for example.

✦ No more feeling that you're a nuisance, an extra responsibility.

✦   No sneers at conversational efforts, after dinner parties.

✦   No more rows over family members.

✦   No sneers at attempts at self-improvement.

✦   No more treatment as a small child.

✦   No more pleading to put up shelves, mow the lawn and take out the rubbish.

✦   The ability to call in professionals to do repair jobs, without massive sulking.

✦   No more keeping the peace in family life.

✦   No more clothes to pick up, wash, or collect from the cleaners.

✦   Staying late at parties.

✦   Meeting new people without put-downs later.

✦   No more pretence that everything is all right.

✦   No more fretful dashes home for *his* arrival.

✦   No more hiding card slips or statements.

CHANGING YOUR SCENERY

Take stock of your life in its entirety – your finances, social life, friends, family and responsibilities. Make a list of your assets – from looks and sexual attraction to your talents, such as cooking, organisation and homemaking. Get an overall picture of what you have to offer. Then write down what you need – in practical and emotional terms. Be really honest with yourself – no one has to see your musings.

Work out your options: could you, or should you, finalise your legal position? How long would it take to sort out legal and financial affairs? How many other people are involved in the process? How supportive will they be? Could you sell stock, or your home, if this is a sensible option? Gather together all the relevant papers, tax forms, insurance and assurance policies you can muster for the time when you seek advice. What are your options in terms of life roles? Are your children dependent enough for you to primarily be a mother – and do you want that as your chief role? Are you a devoted grandmother, or carer? How long will your skills realistically be needed, and what will happen when they are not in demand?

Get advice: ideally, seek out a professional. Friends and family may be loving and over-optimistic, or concerned with settling old scores. They may also have an interest in preserving you in the status quo, which may not be in your best interests. Get ready, with facts and figures, to have a professional work on some life planning with you – including looking at just how sensible your plans and hopes are, and if they could damage your financial interests in the long term.

Weigh up the pros and cons, and then *decide*. The very act of making a decision can set a chain of motion into action. Even if your ideals seem unlikely, start working towards them. Put in that mortgage application. Talk to a solicitor. Draw up the papers. Ask the estate agent to call. Decisiveness moves you forward, while dithering depresses and immobilises.

To start yourself off on that first step, you'll need some support and advice, and it will come from your own supply of advisors, your support network.

SUPPORT NETWORK

Your doctor: should be someone to whom you feel you can really talk, about emotional as well as physical problems. If you have recently moved, or a surgery change is in the offing, then this may be the time for an assessment.

Ask yourself:

✦ How does your doctor feel about new views and treatments, about alternative medicine? What about flexibility of approach and second opinions?

✦ How old is your doctor? Apart from the generation gap, what will happen when your doctor retires? Is there another one at the practice or in the locality whose list you can join – or would you simply be "added on" somewhere?

✦ What about availability of appointments? How difficult is it to get one?

✦ What about longer slots, for occasions when you want to talk as well as consult?

✦ What is emergency cover like? Home visits?

✦ What about the consultants used by your doctor? Is he prepared to do some research on your behalf, and offer you a choice or views and styles, or is it simply a case of attending as tradition dictates?

✦ How does your doctor feel about a patient who asks questions, demurs and wants full information, in detail, on all aspects of care? Is such a patient dismissed as "difficult"?

Your accountant: will be vital, as divorce settlements, separation agreements, pension planning, property dealings and legacies all have tax implications. If you don't have your own accountant, start by asking friends and self-employed acquaintances, so you have some names and perhaps introductions to start with. An accountant who looks after your interests fully will not only be able to save you payments of unnecessary tax – even with self-assessment – but also advise you on allowances and perhaps recommend a financial advisor. Check fees, and remember that the better kept your accounts, the less time will have to be spent preparing your submissions, and the cheaper the advice in the long run.

Your solicitor: will help with property transactions, wills and agreements – plus, of course, any vital divorce agreements and settlements. It's vital to have a solicitor who makes you feel understood, and who doesn't bombard you with legalese, or at the other extreme, write you off as a silly, uninformed female. However, be aware that you will pay for that listening ear, so restrict your calls to legal consequences of your situation, rather than using your solicitor as an expensive counsellor.

Your financial advisor: can also be your accountant, if he is independent, without existing links to insurance/assurance companies or building societies. You should plan to discuss everything financial: from pensions to budgeting and shares to tax savings, with your financial adviser, who can direct you on to relevant advice. If you find the mere thought of such sessions boring and depressing, consider going to a woman advisor. She will not only understand your situation, but also perhaps be able to open your eyes to the importance and satisfaction of being in charge of your finances, rather than dominated by them.

Your friendly neighbour: who will take in messages, hold spare keys, pick up post when you're away, and call the emergency services if you're ill. The fortunate few make such good friends with their neighbours that a virtual extended family results. You, of course, will reciprocate fully.

Your nearest (and perhaps dearest) friends, ideally of the "foul weather" variety: You need to keep on hand the telephone number of a friend who you can ring when you're laid low by illness, bad news, or tragedy such as bereavement. Obviously, that's not the only time you'll be in contact, but there may be times when one of you will have an increased dependency and vulnerability. Then, you'll need someone familiar who can provide tea and sympathy, collect groceries when you're ill, feed your pets and water your plants, and be non-judgmental about the state of your kitchen. It is, of course, a prerequisite that such a paragon lives near enough to make all this possible.

Your mechanic: who is a necessity in order to stay confidently mobile. You clearly have to be able to trust your mechanic – who may be part of a large service team, or in charge of a small, oily business. It's as important that he communicates well – and doesn't sneer at your attempts to describe that rattle or engine whine. Your mechanic should be able to get you spare parts cheaply, be prepared to fit you in when emergency strikes and will come out in the event of a breakdown (until you join that motoring association, of course!) It also helps if he treats you as knowing as much about engines as the next man – a good sign is the presence of a number of women customers, who stay with him or her.

Your counsellor/religious advisor/therapist: The very idea of such people may make you uneasy, rather than anxious to add them to your life. Cynics sometimes say that you're really hiring a parent when you see a counsellor. You get undivided attention, uninterrupted time to express your feelings and support, as well as insight into why you behave as you do. It could be argued that you could get all that from good chums. The problem is that friends inevitably have their own agendas, and can't really be objective about your behaviour. There is also the fact that we sometimes feel guilty about hogging the limelight for too long – a problem might not be expressed as fully as you might like with a friend.

With a professional, however, you can harp on for as long as you like – you're paying for it, after all. Professionals also have contacts, access and useful suggestions for help and advice that you might never have heard of. So, whilst the whole idea of visiting such a person might be a touch too self-indulgent for your tastes, don't dismiss the prospect out of hand.

If you really can't take to the idea of therapy or advice, then consider another American idea that has gained some British converts – your own Tough Love Group. If you have good friends in your area, you might arrange for a regular gathering – weekly or monthly – in one home. Everyone sits around a table, and each person has the chance to talk about a problem, ranging from finances, infidelity and drugs, to redundancy and ageing parents. She can say *exactly* what she likes, and is listened to without interruptions. There is one proviso – *nothing* said ever leaves the confines of the room and the shared feelings act as their own insurance policies.

So much for theory – but how do we put that theory into practice? Here are the stories of four women who fought back from – and through – life-change, which wasn't of their own making. Their successes don't minimise the difficulties involved. No matter how easy those changes appeared, all the women experienced hurt, trauma, fear, insecurity, moments of panic, illness and decimated confidence and self-esteem. Yet all of them feel that they have grown, changed and increased in confidence through the process – and all say that their new lives bring them great satisfaction and feelings of accomplishment.

Noelle

Noelle was the wife of a City man – with a home in the stockbroker belt, and a settled, apparently idyllic life with children, dogs, a lovely home and lifestyle. She had no financial worries and a pleasant social

life – with all the perks of life enjoyed by the family of
a successful man – including a small London pied-a-
terre. When the marriage broke up, however, everything changed.

Noelle found that her husband had excellent
financial advice, and that she didn't even know what
questions to ask the advisors she was recommended
to consult. Life became a stressful round of visits to
financiers, accountants and solicitors. She had to
deal with the complexities of family trust, and the
fact that much of her husband's money was now in
offshore accounts.

Her husband wanted to live nearby – with his mis-
tress – a fact that not only embittered and humiliat-
ed Noelle, but also made any sort of settled lifestyle
within her existing circle very difficult. Fees and
costs involved in dealing with finances were eating
into capital reserves, so after a few months, Noelle
decided to cut her losses – partly for the sake of her
health, and also for her children's financial security.
Against her advisors' advice she agreed to the sale of
the family home – and the London pied-a-terre.
Provision was made which would give her an
allowance – in her fifties, she was also very concerned about her lack of good pension coverage. She
put her capital into a small, one-bedroom London
flat, in a good location, and sold virtually all her possessions. Her dogs went to friends, and her colour-
co-ordinated wardrobe went to designer sales.

Before, Noelle would have donated to charity, but
now she wanted and needed every penny she could
get! She cut her hair, put in highlights, bought a tiny
capsule wardrobe from sales and discount stores,
and furnished her flat solely from antique markets,
auctions and even car-boot sales – all new experiences for her. She now does day and evening courses, enjoys all the free tours and lectures the muse-
ums and galleries offer, and has got to know a wide
circle of people of all ages through charity work. She

is still worried about her financial future and health cover. She still feels occasional fear and anger about her lost secure and comfortable life. But she feels better for cutting all ties, and is changing, with the help of women's groups, self-help books and the constant change and stimulation she knew she needed and would get from her new life.

Mary

When Mary was widowed in her early forties, life in her provincial town changed completely. Her husband's financial provisions were enough to ensure her children's future, but would have meant a humiliating drop in standards in their old circle. Friends rallied round, but Mary found the reduced standard in her lifestyle not just embarrassing – in terms of shopping and hunting for second-hand clothes and cheaper food – but stressful. She knew that she would have to get a job. She had worked as a nurse, some twenty years before, and knew that her skills would have to be updated.

She knew that no moves should be made immediately after a stressful loss of life, and remained in her village for a year, making economies, and allowing her children to take exams. Then, against all advice, she sold their home, and invested her capital for growth rather than income. She had re-trained, and was amazed when she got a job nursing in a nearby county town – preferable to working in her old village, where the changes would have been too stressful, socially and emotionally. She couldn't afford to buy a home on her income, and rented an old, rundown flat, which she cleaned, decorated and furnished from auctions and market stalls. Her children, now of course at university, hated it, and were resentful about their old home being sold. In-laws felt the same, and Mary battled with inferences of selfishness, as well as insecurity and fear.

But a few years on, she feels that she instinctively made the right decision. Her children have their own lives, and she has won a grudging respect from them – horrified as they were by her return to work. She has achieved career success on her own and her life is free from any taint of charity and friends' largesse – as well as memories of the old days. Mary now runs her own finances – after costly mistakes, finding the whole process "a huge learning curve". Her new life is so busy she has little time to brood. There is no romance, although she would at some stage like a man in her life. But now, she's considering sub-letting her flat and finding some contract work abroad, perhaps in the Middle East. She is too busy to look back, although the process of grieving, and dealing with shock, upheaval and financial insecurity has left its mark. She tries, however, to look on the experience as a long-term blessing in disguise.

Mari

Mari faced drastic and sudden changes when her husband's business went into liquidation, and bankruptcy followed. The relationship came under considerable strain, not helped by the attitude of his children from an earlier marriage, who felt that in some way, Mari had created the conditions which led to the failure of the business. They moved to a council house on the outskirts of the city in which they once enjoyed a secluded and pleasant lifestyle in a leafy suburb. To Mari, it felt like a descent into hell. Her husband became isolated, and started to drink, and unknown to her, began to suffer from depression. Money was a constant worry. Gone were extras like private health care – and even mobility. A rusty unreliable car constantly broke down, and public transport was almost non-existent.

After a few months, Mari's gnawing fear overcame her depression, and she realised that she had better help herself, as otherwise, she would lose all control of her life. She scheduled her days, and fitted in trips to the local, underused but helpful library. As well as reading countless self-help books, she developed an interest in healthy food, largely to safeguard her own health. Occasional, humiliating contact with old friends led to "repayment" through some healthy baking for coffee mornings and jumble sales. People liked her food, but Mari knew that she couldn't cook commercially, due to health regulations about kitchens.

But several people were happy to have her cook in their homes, and whilst there, Mari heard how difficult it was for them to get cleaning women. So, she filled the rusty car with supermarket-bought materials and equipment, and set off. Her rota gradually increased, and she eventually earned enough to part-rent a suitable kitchen – and could start to sell to local health food stores. She still cleans in addition to the cooking, and has been able to come off benefit. She eats better, feels in control of her life, and looks forward to expanding her catering business. She doesn't know for how long – or if her marriage will last; her husband has become an isolated depressive drunk, but her work helps Mari to feel some sense of control in her life.

Anna

Anna retired early to care for her ageing mother. When her mother died Anna felt worn-out and isolated, despite the concern of her family. She was left their home, and had kept up pension payments, so had only a modest income. After a spell at a luxurious health farm – to her family's amazement, she shocked them further by declining a home with any of them. Against their advice, she also decided to sell her home, and buy a small, easy-care one-bedroom flat. Relatives young and old proffered advice constantly –

interior design issues through to financial planning
would be too much for her, she was assured – she
needed to rest. She refused offers of pets after her
mother died – again to her family's horror, who felt
she needed the company.

After a couple of assertiveness courses, and self-
development seminars, Anna got some new financial
advisors, and astounded everyone by announcing
that instead of the quiet life her family envisioned for
her, she wanted to travel. She needed to make a
home with one of them, she was told – built in grandchildren to care for, who loved her. But newly confident, Anna announced that she was only in her early
sixties, and wanted to do some living at last. Her
short trips went well, and she then announced that
she wanted to travel around the world. Yet again, she
met protestations – she was too unworldly and inno-
cent to be able to cope. But she planned carefully,
and had a wonderful experience, coping with minor
problems and illnesses. She has now decided, having
made a variety of friends in America, that she will
sub-let her flat for three or four months a year, and
travel for that time. Her budget will just about balance, and her future looks promising.

CHAPTER TWO:
COPING WITH CHANGE

If you were offered the chance to feel happier and freer, to save – or earn some money, to increase your living space, reduce stress and increase your opportunities – free, in the privacy of your home, no drugs retail or selling therapy involved, would you be interested? It's available to everyone, and it's called "getting rid of stuff". No drug connotations here – but some addictions might be cured in the process.

SIMPLIFICATION

What is "stuff"? It's what we fill our homes and lives with. Stuff is furniture, collectibles, equipment, knick-knacks, souvenirs, memorabilia and clothes – junk – you get the idea. Stuff has to be housed, insured, dusted, worried over and valued. When we get too much of it, we move to a larger space – to collect more stuff. We worry about it being burgled – and sometimes don't even like to travel or go on holiday because stuff is so important to us. Life changes, job opportunities and smaller desirable residences can be passed over because of stuff. Ask yourself – do you *really* need more space in your home – or just less stuff?

That's merely the physical variety of stuff. Our lives can also be clogged and cluttered by attitudes and beliefs that we also cling to. Bitterness, resentment, anger, self-pity and hopelessness can have a similar emotional effect as can cupboards and drawers over-filled with unused and broken junk. So can draining friendships and total muddle in your life.

Modern thinking on stress control and mild depression often includes suggestions on simplifying life as part of dealing with the conditions. It makes sense that we feel better, more in control of our lives and more hopeful when we are in ordered surroundings. Even if you don't believe in Eastern philosophies, such as Feng Shui, it is easy to understand that clutter, over-stuffed cupboards and general disorder adds to a feeling of tiredness, dejection and lack of control or direction; whilst harmony and order lift our spirits.

Is less really more?

Even if you remained convinced that a tidy home is the sign of a wasted life, and that fulfilled living is a messy, untidy business, give some thought to the idea that your living might be more fulfilled with less effort and time wasting involved in everyday matters. If you are a natural hoarder, possessions may symbolise security, permanence and home. It's true that minimalism is not for everyone, but is your stuff simply mooring you – or anchoring you in place?

Possessions aren't only about security of course; they are also closely linked to status. For many people, simplifying their life or "downshifting" is linked with reduced circumstances and a less materialistic view of life. All very worthy for those who wish to develop alternative styles of living, but not always for the rest of us. Getting rid of stuff can be a part of such a changed lifestyle, but it can also allow you to live even better with a few well-chosen and beautiful pieces, rather than a collection of possessions in need of repair, irrelevant, or just there from force of habit.

Reducing possessions can also save you money, thus freeing it up of the acquisition of pieces and experiences that you really want in your life. You will have more choice about where you live when your "stuff" doesn't dictate square footage requirements. Insurance cover – and perhaps even security systems can also be simplified and reduced in cost. If you have been a collector, you can either develop a new interest, or learn to visit art galleries, auction rooms and great collections in the knowledge that someone else is housing, insuring, dusting and worrying over such beautiful objects.

Then there are opportunities open to those less shackled with possessions. You have a chance to ensure that your treasured possessions go to the intended recipient, who will really appreciate and treasure them. There's nothing like clearing out someone's estate after death to learn about how the best laid schemes of donors can go amiss. You'll also have a chance to utilise inheritance and gift tax regulations to your benefit – and then to develop your own taste in interiors.

Should it stay or should it go?

Do you even know how much stuff you have – is it secreted on top of wardrobes, under the bed, in suitcases, hot presses and in the attic? Professional home and wardrobe weeders apply a few rules:

✦ When was the last time you wore or used it?

✦ If it is supposed to be valuable – how recently has it been valued?

✦ If you've kept it "just in case", or felt that "it might come in useful" – were you right?

✦ If you inherited it, or were given it as a well-meant gift – how long is long enough for it to stay with you?

✦ If it's too good to throw away, why aren't you using it?

✦ Why are you paying for other people's storage problems?

The first step is to sort and box or bag the unwanted stuff. One tip from the professionals – if you really can't decide, and feel very uneasy at the idea of parting, put the stuff in a black bag, and keep it for a few weeks. If, at the end of the time you set yourself, you can't remember what's in the bag without checking – you don't need it. The same applies if you feel that you're really holding on to your past life along with some clutter – clothes, children's toys, photographs, furniture. Be honest with yourself about why you want to hang on to stuff you never use.

If you have more of other people's clutter than your own, then learn the lesson about taking more in when asked in the future. It can help to set a deadline – six months to a year, and make it clear that the sofa/trunk/suitcases will be history after expiry.

If there is stuff that you genuinely can't get rid of for a variety of reasons – legal, financial etc., then think about clearing out one room in your house, and using it solely for properly packed storage. If you want to move, would it be easier and cheaper to consider storage, whilst you live in a similar home?

Asset stripping

If you have a much-appreciated item which is hardly used in your present life, and which uses up space, concern and insurance money, think about passing it on to whosoever you would like to have it after your death. Some things, no matter how valuable, simply cannot be sold, so why not ensure "a good home" now?

Research local auction houses and antique dealers. If you have any photographs of your stuff, bring them along for an idea of their value *right now*. Remember that if you sell this way, you will have to pay transport charges, plus the commission taken by the dealer.

Alternatively, consider taking your stuff along to a car boot sale. It can be amazing what people will pay out large sums for – there might be a lack of interest in those little silver frames, but brisk haggling over your long unwanted floral dinner service, anniversary present.

Think about holding a charity auction with morning coffee in your home for a few friends – or even your neighbours. Or suggest the idea of a community "clear-out jumble sale", with teenage daughters of chums modelling some of the clothes. The more enterprising could involve local design students to re-model some clothes for charity auction.

Donate to charity shops – but don't overlook refuges, shelters for the homeless, pensioners' groups and overseas aid organisations. Many organisations will collect donations, but if not, club together with some friends and do a few runs as a group to give you the feeling that someone will benefit from your efforts.

You will inevitably have to make a few visits to the local dump, or maybe hire a skip, but before you toss away old family momentoes, think about collectors of such items. Is there a museum, private collection or collection that might appreciate, or even put on display your old swords, top hat and tails, or antique lace and Victorian underwear?

DESIGNS ON YOUR WARDROBE

One of the biggest bonuses in simplifying your wardrobe is the opportunity to replace it with a few well-chosen pieces. If you have a lasting love of designer clothes, a little lateral thinking can indulge it creatively, according to the professional stylists and shoppers. Cultivate a young designer. Contact a local college of fashion, or simply go along to a student designer show. Or contact a lecturer, many of whom would be happy to see idealistic students getting in some practice at commercial creations. When you do find one whose style you like, make sure that you both understand and agree on the price, and also the length of time you are prepared to wait for your creation. Experts advise checking the cost of fabric – many youthful designers become restless when faced with commercial restrictions, and also the finish of the garment. Look carefully at seams, hems and linings.

Some young designers are prepared to subsidise their own work by making creative and skilled updates and alterations to clients' existing wardrobes. Look again at your favourite designer or expensive outfits. Could the shoulders, the waist or the jacket length be altered to update a classic? Could the style be updated, or could a new skirt be made or bought to give a favourite the current style essentials? A surprising number of ladies-who-lunch, dine and socialise, up-date their wardrobes in this way, so don't dismiss it out of hand as a means of creating your own slightly-worn collections.

The same philosophy can be used with your accessories. Keep an eye open for jewellers and designers who work with fabrics and metals, and might re-make or re-string slightly outdated jewellery. Update your watches by unusual straps – fabric, metal or cloth. Don't overlook hats. Many perfectly good (and flattering) ones make their way to jumble sales because of a current trend. Here also, keep an eye out for hat makers and stylists in your area.

Perhaps your hat simply needs a high crown, which can easily be done by skilled cutting and insertions. Perhaps it is crumpled, or needs a new circumference wire. Work out if it would make financial sense to have a favoured and flattering hat updated professionally.

Professional wardrobe consultants advise thinking laterally and also very creatively whilst shopping. If you're slim, don't overlook youthful high fashion stores – just be aware of the full possibilities of one outfit. A pretty mini dress in your size could become a tunic, or slim fitting top, to be worn over trousers.

Don't neglect the possibilities of antique evening accessories. Beaded lacy chokers, 1930s/40s/50s bags, fabric belts and cocktail hats are just a few items which can be altered, by you or a professional, to develop your own designer style.

When is a bargain not a bargain? When it doesn't fit, or when you wouldn't have bought it at its original price – no matter what. However, sometimes bargains can be missed, due to short sightedness. If you find *the* perfect evening dress, special occasion dress or top that fit, are the right price, shape and style, but may have one feature wrong – think creatively. For example, you may hate sleeveless dresses, or feel that an evening skirt is just too short for your legs. If it's perfect in other respects, including price, think about whether your tailor or designer could make a slinky evening jacket in a matching or toning colour, or could add on lacy or toning sleeves. If a skirt is too short, could it take a false hem, in a deeper colour, or luxurious fabric inset? Could a dress be shortened to hip level to fit over a flowing and draped skirt? Learn to look at clothes in a more open-minded way, and with a skilled designer or tailor, you could create some individual styles for yourself.

The well-advertised and attended designer sales may provide good value and even some bargains for the dedicated. For many of us, however, they can also be over-priced, over-crowded and over-stressed. Look into a girlie outing to one of the specialist discount stores or even villages. Invest in *Wear to be Seen*, an excellent directory of dress agencies throughout England and Wales. Compiled by Sue Tunnard, it is invaluable for the designer fan. Contact her at 67, Little Lane, Docking, Kings Lynn, Norfolk, Tel. 01485 518000.

If you travel to New York, Paris, Rome, Milan or Berlin, ask about the shops which handle end-of-season designer wear, which may be a season out of date, but at those prices – who cares?

Watch the catwalks, aim for style, rather than trends, and plan for your basics to last several years. Check if designs are tailored or loose, if trousers are important, if skirts are short or long, if jackets are long, fitted or padded, if design is monochrome, colourful or all-contrasting colour, if shoes or boots are worn, and how make-up and accessories are worn.

Laurel Herman holds one to one consultations, seminars and workshops on make-overs and confidence building. She has a specialist interest in the topic of women facing challenges such as recovery or life-change. Consultations include Positive Presence sessions. Contact her at 18a Lambolle Place, London, NW3 4PG, Tel. 0207 586 7925.

DEALING WITH STRESS AND EMOTIONS

Clutter isn't only found in junk-filled cupboards. Fears, beliefs and attitudes can clutter up our lives as well, and even help to create unwanted stress. Taking responsibility for your personal care and safety can be as much a part of simplifying your life as a de-junking your loft. Do you know about your body's danger signs?

+ Chest pain/discomfort.

+ Unusual shortness of breath, or a persistent cough.

+ Recurrent and inexplicable dizziness.

+ Weight loss – with no changed eating patterns/diets involved.

+ Unusual digestive changes.

+ Notable change in bladder or bowel habits.

+ Blood in the stools.

+ Any other unexplained bleeding, or a vaginal discharge.

✦ A sore that will not heal.

✦ A mole that changes in colour, size or texture, or bleeds.

✦ Unexplained and persistent back pain.

BODY MAINTENANCE

Here are a few suggestions to help keep your body in tip-top condition:

✦ **Breast checks** – self is best, learn from an expert, and check once a month.

✦ **Mammogram** – ask about a base mammogram at 40, and then every two years or so. Over 50, on your doctor's advice, consider it once a year.

✦ **Cervical smear** – once every two years, at a time when you are free of any infection.

✦ **Gynaecological examination** – with checks for ovarian and uterine abnormality – once every two years.

✦ **Bone scan** – for osteoporosis vulnerability – once every two years, unless your doctor advises more often.

✦ **Moles** – any changes, e.g. thickening, enlargement, itching, weeping, colour change.

✦ **Eyes** – once a year.

LIFE EVENT RATING SCALE

Holmes and Rahe developed the life event rating scale in 1967. They claim that if during the course of a year you accumulate a score of more than 300 points, your chance of a serious health problem developing in the next two years is more than 80 per cent.

Should your score lie between 150 and 300 points, you have a 50 per cent chance of serious illness in the next two years. The risk drops to 33 per cent for a score of below 150 points.

Life Event	Scale
Death of spouse	100
Divorce	73
Marital separation	65
Prison or mental hospital confinement	63
Death of a close family member	63
Major injury/illness	53
Marriage	50
Being fired	47
Marital reconciliation	45
Retirement	45
Major change in health or behaviour of a family member	44
Pregnancy	40
Sexual difficulties	39
Adding to family (e.g. through birth, adoption, 'oldies' moving in)	39
Major business readjustments	39
Major change in financial state	38
Death of a close friend	36
Changing line of work	36
Major change in number of arguments with spouse	35
Taking on mortgage purchasing home, business etc.	31
Foreclosure on a mortgage or loan	30
Major change in job responsibility	29
Son/daughter leaving home	29

In-law trouble   29
Outstanding personal achievement   28
Wife beginning/ceasing work outside home   26
Beginning/ceasing formal schooling   26
Major change in living conditions   25
Revision of personal habits   24
Troubles with the boss   23
Major change in working hours/conditions   20
Change in residence   20
Changing to a new school   20
Major change in recreation   19
Major change in church activities   19
Major changes in social activities   18
Taking on loans less than £10,000   17
Major change in sleeping habits   16
Major change in number of family get togethers   15
Major change in eating habits   15
Holidays   13
Christmas   12
Minor violations of law   11

Source: T. H. Holmes and R. H. Rahe, The Social Re-adjustments Rating Scale, *Journal of Psycho-somatic Research*, (1967) V11, pp. 213-18.

HOW TO CHANGE

Prepare

Assess your values, and decide exactly what you want to change. Will there be a conflict of important values? Sometimes, it's necessary to give one value priority, even if it means letting others temporarily slide.

Plan

How much time will you *really* need? It can take much longer than you think to lose the unwanted from your life, be it weight, a partner or an attitude. The (apparently) impossible takes longer. Assess what might be involved – perhaps losses, such as fun, a sense of belonging, respect, status and even money. You have to be sure that your changes *will* work, and will be worthwhile in the long term in order to see them through.

Know that what can go wrong, will

How will you cope? Making things as easy as possible, e.g. if you're trying to lose weight, don't have a fridge full of fattening foods. Take it in small steps, and forgive yourself for slips – there's always another chance – the only failure is giving up in despair.

Use the proven method of visualisation and reward

It helps to use this motivational method to encourage your progress. In a battle between imagination and will, imagination wins every time. So use it. Picture how you will look, feel and act when you've changed. Use affirmations, and write out a "contract" with yourself – see appendix for details. Concentrate on your goals and plan – make them part of your life *now*.

STAGES OF CHANGE

These can be compared to the process of climbing a mountain. You start off with *the fantasy* at base camp – all seems possible, and you're filled with hope. *Trench warfare,* however, sets in, as you dig in to battle with the elements of change, and realise that there is no one else – you have to rely on yourself. *The ascent* can be varied. There can be steep climbs, with stress and worry involved, and the fear that you've taken on more than you can cope with. There can be *crevasses*, when you feel hurt and despairing, and feel like giving up. There can be long periods of *plateaux* ascent, when you feel that nothing much is happening, and boredom can be a real threat. But finally, you reach *the summit* – and after coming to terms with initial elation, you may realise that you don't feel at all like you expected you would – and start to worry about where you go from here. You may then realise that change is in fact an ongoing process.

GOAL SETTING

Effective goal setting is a vital part of change. Dr. Aidan Moran, a psychologist who advises the Irish Olympic Team, is an expert in motivation under pressure – although he doubtless would prefer the term "challenge" to pressure. Winners plan, losers worry – and blame, he feels. Mental toughness, which marks out the champions, involves staying in the moment. Focusing and planning rather than worrying and despairing. The key is to focus on per-formance, rather than results.

Goals, according to Aidan Moran, should fit five requirements for success, using the SMART objec-tive/goal-setting method. For example, setting goals for your life could be:

✦   *Specific*: start by inviting three or four friends for a meal/drink/coffee – whatever you feel comfortable with.

✦   *Measurable*: you can organise the event, plan and put it into action, and gauge later how you felt it went, and you coped.

✦   *Achievable*: with effort and planning on your part – cleaning, shopping, preparation and developing hostess skills. It is a goal that you could, with effort, reasonably expect to meet.

✦ *Realistic*: don't aim for a large party, that would be expensive, difficult to organise, and daunting to cope with, plus depressing if you couldn't get enough people to attend on the night in question. A modest party is a good start, will develop social skills and contacts, and has a good chance of success. Give your friends – and you might have to ask six, to allow for other commitments – plenty of notice, and avoid public holidays, etc.

✦ *Time based*: you will set a date well in advance.

According to psychologists, goals involved in creating a new life after major and perhaps painful changes should include:

✦ Keeping busy and active with productive work – paid or for the benefits of others.

✦ Ensuring that you have a good network of social support, ensuring that you see your friends regularly. Have lunch with pals at least once a week – even a sandwich will suffice. Try to go out with friends on another evening each week – to someone's home, or to a film, play or community meeting.

✦ Developing your own career/interest based network. This helps you to keep your circle of friends up to date, and allows for the gaps when friends move away, or aren't available during holidays, weekends etc.

✦ Working on developing an outgoing personality. Read up on self-help books on dealing with problems and overcoming losses and setback.

✦ Getting some organisation into your life. Simplify, learn to make lists and keep your business affairs in order to cut down on the need for crisis management.

✦ Aiming to stay healthy. Take plenty of exercise even if you can't afford to join a health club. Stick to a healthy diet, including regular meals. Allow time for relaxation – whether it's yoga, relaxation tapes or meditation. Relaxation is now built into programmes for stress reduction and helps to build up your physical health.

✦ Learning to be more optimistic and confident about your abilities and developing your confidence, even if at times you have to fake it till you make it. Stop worrying – list all the times you wasted time, opportunities for fun and celebration whilst worrying unnecessarily over something that never happened.

✦ Staying open to new ideas and opportunities, rather than insisting that the values, standards and beliefs with which you grew up are now as relevant and ideal as they once were.

✦ Seeking out some psychological support for you. If you're fortunate enough to have trusted and nearby girl friends, relaxed – or even emotional – chats around the kitchen table may provide all the empathy and care that you need. If you're alone, don't rule out professional support. Part of taking care of you is recognising that sometimes we need to ask for help – and that sometimes we are our own worst enemies.

THREE WOMEN MOVING FORWARD

If clearing attics and store cupboards is one way of getting rid of stuff, getting rid of a fear is another way of moving forward, as well as a great confidence booster. Breaking through what may seem trivial fears can provoke lasting effects.

Joan

Joan had never seen herself as a fit or athletic person, rather as fragile or physically inept. Divorced and bereft in her fifties, she dates her recovery "from the day I climbed a mountain. Okay, so it really only was a very large hill, but it was marked on the map as a mountain – and I checked it in the atlas." Although initially appalled at the suggestion she agreed to go walking with friends. "I was so tired, and it took about four hours, with breaks. My legs ached, and it was suggested a few times that I turned back – I must have looked awful. My calf muscles ached, I thought I would have a heart attack – but when I got to the summit – well, it wasn't just the view. I felt I had done something I would *never* have thought myself capable of – and it did wonders for me."

Jill

Jill took up the unexpected opportunity of a round on an assault course on a corporate weekend. "I'd always secretly admired women who went on outward-bound type courses, like that Julie Walters film, but I'd never had the courage. I walked over tree stumps, across bars, shinned up nets, squeezed through tyres and swung across ponds. There wasn't time to be scared – although I was when my arms gave out on a Tarzan type swing across a pond. Next time round, I was under pressure – but in the end, it *did* give me more confidence in my capabilities – she who can climb up a net can do almost any type of thing."

Kirsty

Once widowed, Kirsty discovered that her terror of flying would leave her isolated and lonely in her small community. "So I took a fear of flying course. It *was* as bad as I had thought – I was scared sick, but I kept on, and kept saying to myself, I *can* deal with this degree of turbulence. In fact I even found myself comforting others during the flight. They were marvellous on the course, so kind to us. I won't ever enjoy flying, but I have worked my way up to three-hour flights, and I hope to try the States next. It really has made a huge difference to my life."

Still need to be convinced?

SORTING OUT THE CLUTTER

You would be truly amazed at the amount of clutter one person can accumulate. You may have to be fairly innovate with the sale of some items, and hard on yourself – but it will be worthwhile.

One woman's clutter provided the following:

A Round the world airline ticket/trip-	from the sale of an Old Master
A designer outfit in the sales-	from selling two wardrobes of clothes
A course in philosophy -	from dumping unsupportive friends
Regular visits to country pals-	no replacement for a deceased pet
'Antiquing' friends and trips-	from giving away antiques to children
Eurostar First Class to Paris-	from savings on insurance policy
Art classes-	from sale of mahogany chest
One bedroomed sea view apartment-	from sale of mansion with debts and draughts
Space for friends to visit-	from removal of children's possessions
Yoga and relaxation classes-	from dealing with depression over a dead relationship
An organic vegetable garden-	from sale of a sun dial wedding present
New friends and hobby-	from donation of plaque to museum
Income from student letting-	space clearing of ex-husband's junk

There are some very useful books, which can help
you cope with change and health.

Health/stress reading list

Arnot, B. (1999) *The Breast Cancer Prevention Diet*,
   (Newleaf, Dublin)
Blackman, H. (1997) *How to Look and Feel Half Your
   Age for the Rest of Your Life*, (Virgin, London)
Burns, D. (1990) *The Feel Good Handbook*, (Penguin,
   New York)
Carlson, R. (1998) *Don't Sweat the Small Stuff*,
   (Hodder & Stoughton, London)
Chopra, D. (1993) *Ageless Body, Timeless Mind*,
   (Rider Ebury Press, London)
Coleman, D. (1996) *Emotional Intelligence*,
   (Bloomsbury, London)
Fairly, J. & Stacey, S. (1998) *Feel Fabulous Forever*,
   (Kyle Cathie, London)
Glenville, M. (2000) *Natural Alternatives to HRT
   Cookbook*, (Kyle Cathie, London)
Holden, R. (1998) *Happiness Now*, (Hodder &
   Stoughton, London)
Holford, P. (1997) *The Optimum Nutrition Bible*,
   (Piatkus, London)
Jeffers, R. (1991) *Feel the Fear and Do It Anyway*,
   (Rider Random House, London)
Kenton, L. (1995) *The New Ageless Woman*,
   (Vermilion, London)
Kenton, L. (1998) *10 Steps to a New You*, (Rider
   Ebury Press, London)
Stoppard M. (1994) *Menopause*, (Dorling Kindersley,
   London)

CHAPTER THREE:
FINANCE

Still waiting for your financial prince to come? Or do you feel more like you've been left the debts of a deposed monarch? As with so many things, we often don't understand how much of a key enabler money is – until the supply threatens to dry up. This can show up in the larger, important life issues, such as mortgages, incomes, debts and pensions. It can also be cruelly felt in smaller ways – do you still want to go to the theatre if you have to think about the cost of a taxi, or ordered car afterwards? Making your own travel arrangements, and waiting around for check-in in economy is a very different travel experience to relaxing in the comfort of a business class lounge with a partner.

What about wedding presents? Charity donations? Club subscriptions? Are they still financially justifiable? Then there's the sick feeling when bills thud onto the mat and the chill when you hear another example of ageism and longer retirement periods in the future. Yes, money equals power, and comparative powerlessness will come as a profound shock for a woman who has previously not taken *full* financial responsibility for her life.

An added problem is that each of us – including men, sees money in different ways, and responds to different financial "buttons" being pushed. For example, if the chips were down, where would your priorities lie?

✦   In ensuring your children's future, financially and educationally?

✦   In creating future security – paying off all debts, and avoiding future borrowing?

✦   In maintaining your status – home, lifestyle, with draconian private economies?

✦   In ensuring you had the freedom and indepen-
dence never to be reliant again?

The same amount of money can do any of those. The
important thing is to know your priorities – and why,
so that you can plan wisely, whether you're a cash-
a-holic or a moneyrexic, and avoid the mistakes
made by other women.

According to a top financial advisor, the following
are the commonest mistakes made by women
unused to money management:

1. **Women all too often assume that their current
marital status is permanent.** Hence, the changing
states, financially speaking, of marriage, desertion,
separation, divorce or widowhood comes as a nasty
shock to those with little understanding of the implications. Women sometimes fail to understand the
changes in tax, insurance policies, pensions, mortgages and joint accounts that changes in status may
bring.

2. **Women all too often have said "Oh, I leave all
that to my husband/partner", and persist in the
illusion, sometimes sadly delusion, that when it
comes to financial difficulties, ignorance is
bliss.** If they can't understand, they won't have to –
until they have no choice.

3. **Women all too often sign on the dotted line
when requested (or ordered) to do so by their
partners.** Sometimes too scared – or trusting – to ask
for a full explanation, or even a basic one, many find
that they have signed away rights to properties, bonds,
policies, accounts, leases, business shares, etc.

4. **Women often hang on stubbornly to the status
quo – a home, trust fund, land or business,
sometimes from spite, occasionally from fear or**

often from noble motives. Faced with drastic change, many are concerned about children's inheritances or rights being lost or sold, and so refuse to listen to advice. That refusal may have disastrous consequences for years to come.

5. **Women can fear making mistakes, and may be indecisive or over-cautious.** This can result in stagnation in management, and mis-managed funds. Think of the little old lady who came into a fortune, and was so anxious not to lose it that it stayed in the "safety" of a bank deposit account, to be depleted by inflation or low interest rates.

6. **Women sometimes establish a personal, rather than professional relationship with their financial advisor.** This can prove very expensive, in terms of fees for advice given, and also in terms of increased vulnerability. When it is of prime importance to feel understood, and be advised by someone whom they can talk to, some women – and their capital, can become easy prey. How many women have been persuaded to sign on the dotted line by an urban advisor in the pin-stripe suit, who seems a decent chap? In reality, of course, he may be a recently redundant consultant, fired by commission possibilities.

7. **Women fail to learn from men, so are brought up with the cultural belief that they will not have to support themselves financially, nor will one day be prime breadwinners for families.** This fact concentrates the male mind wonderfully, in terms of education, career planning and financial concern.

8. **Financially inexperienced women can be vulnerable to pyramid selling and similar schemes.** Faced with a loss in status, financial insecurity and

perhaps lack of marketable skills, such schemes can appear tempting, especially when a restoration of a former lifestyle appears to be part of the future deal.

9. **Women can, through inexperience and lack of financial planning, deplete valuable capital.** Some invest large amounts in home improvements. Others invest unwisely in a business, sometimes backing a new partner or family member, whilst others dip into capital when faced with debt, rather than getting advice on debt management.

10. **Even when they have assured their security, and invested wisely, some women fail to grasp that they cannot relax and leave their capital to take care of itself.** Many do not understand the principle that if their money is not increasing, there is a risk that it may swiftly decrease in value.

Then there is an entire portfolio of attitudes, which complicate may women's financial attitudes:

✦ "It's not *really* feminine to look after my own money – men like to take care of a woman, and don't want someone who knows more about it than they do..."

✦ "I'll worry about all that – pensions, savings and so on when I'm older. Right now, I just want to have some fun while I still can..."

✦ "The best investment is in yourself – then you'll find someone to look after you..."

It's no wonder, with pockets of such antiquated and untrue thinking around, that the bag lady nightmare is still a common female fear. There may even be some justification. Over 40, women do face extra financial challenges, if not risks. Marital changes aside, illness, children's education, adolescent and youthful ambitions and desires, ailing elderly parents, early job loss – they can all produce extra financial stress.

FINANCIAL FITNESS

Who would seriously consider starting on a long journey without first checking the car's petrol gauge? Yet how many women regularly check their financial equivalent?

Making the most of your assets

Note down all of your assets – which may be more than you realise, for example:

+ Your home – with adjustments for mortgages
+ Insurance/assurance policies
+ Savings bonds
+ Cash in the bank
+ Stocks and shares
+ Property
+ Jewels
+ Car

Next, note down debts – loans, credit card bills, unpaid bills, borrowings, overdrafts, service charges, etc. That will give you a picture of your net worth. Now, work out a cash flow forecast – simplify, by filling in estimated spending.

BASIC FINANCIAL SECURITY

Your own home

This is the first aim, either outright ownership, or achievable by mortgage repayment, with allowances for raising repayments should rates go up. Get advice on whether you should take over repayments yourself, buy out your ex-partner or buy a home out of your capital.

Required insurance cover

This covers *house* and *home* cover, and calls for an up to date valuation of both. It also involves reading the small print of policies carefully and getting advice on how much it would cost to re-build or replace your possessions. It is important that you aren't under insured – if your policy covers you "new for old", do you know exactly how much it would cost to replace everything? Also, check with your broker or company about ensuring that you are covered, e.g. your doors and windows are adequately secured; alarm requirements if you want to claim special rates; and general listing descriptions and even photographs of your named items. Anyone who has blithely assumed full cover – only to read the small print after rejection of claim, will say that a few more questions and a little more understanding can literally save thousands of pounds and even more heartbreak – *and remember to keep up the premiums.*

Health cover

This is vital. Do you know exactly what your cover entitles you to, in terms of treatments, access, locality of hospital, consultant care, psychiatric care and alternative health treatments? How long can you stay in hospital under full cover? Is preventive care, e.g. health screening covered, or discounted? What is the best value level of care for your needs, now that you are the breadwinner?

Critical health cover

Again vital if you work for yourself, or have dependent children. Over the past few years, it has increased in popularity, yet not enough people realise, until they have personal experience, the risk of not having it. If you had a long hospital stay, how would you live, pay the mortgage and bills? Would your career suffer, or could you lose your business? Once again, get advice on the type suited to you – the time elapsed before cover starts, plus illnesses covered will dictate the premium, and perhaps the amount paid out.

Pension plans

More about this in Chapter Four, Divorce, but in general terms, we all know that women lag far behind men when it comes to pension planning. Many rely on their partner to save and provide, and think vaguely in terms of life assurance cover, or the family home as providing an individual pension fund for them. Sometimes, however, policy requirements may not be met, or the cover may not be as full or generous as was thought, or there may be debts or re-payments due on the lump sums involved. Some women don't even understand their financial positions in connection with company pensions, let alone how to safeguard their rights. It is easy to despair when faced with the ever-increasing premiums as you notch up birthdays, but there are packages available which will at least get you started, no matter what your age.

If you suspect that the premiums you could afford to pay would not give you a reasonable pension, then you might want to consider an annuity. Often called life assurance in reverse, it pays out a monthly income, and you lose your lump sum when you die. Obviously, the older you are when you take out an annuity, the better the rates.

Another option for women who have a capital sum and are financially independent with understanding children, is to look into a "home income plan" which turns the value of a home into a regular income for the remainder of a lifetime. Obviously again, full financial advice would be vital before any decisions are made.

Emergency nest egg fund

Another vital part of basic financial security is an emergency nest egg fund, which could keep you solvent, pay bills and maintain you for a few months, at least six, should you face some financial crisis, e.g. illness, family problems, unemployment. This should be easily available, i.e. not in long-term savings, where you would incur penalties if you had to release it.

Freedom from debt

One of the most important aspects of financial security – and one of the most critical for a woman newly on her own, is freedom from debt. It's vital to realise that debt is not a sure sign of personal or financial irresponsibility.

As you will know by now, it can all too easily follow marital problems, separation, family difficulties, illness or unemployment. It can appear gallingly unfair and unjustified, and will always be an added stress to your life, so it's vital to know how to deal with debt effectively.

Firstly, even though it may sound trite, *don't panic*. People have differing debt thresholds – a few thousand pounds may appear as serious debt to one person, but merely a cash-flow problem to another. Obviously you want to be in a position to be able to pay off all of your debts easily, and not be financially irresponsible, but to do so effectively, you have to be able to view the situation calmly, and as a whole.

So, the first stage is that classic piece of advice – open up *all* those brown envelopes and list exactly what you owe and when.

Work out, with help if necessary, which are your worst debts, i.e. your most expensive. Your credit card accounts? Overdraft? Would it be cheaper to pay one off in a lump sum, rather than smaller amounts to a range of creditors?

Contact the companies involved as soon as possible, and explain the situation. It may be possible to arrange regular payments, over a period of months. However, ignoring the bills or mentally deferring payment until you can juggle the full amount rarely works, and can result in stern letters often mentioning legal consequences.

Don't go to the other extreme either, and opt for larger re-payments than you can afford to maintain. Otherwise, you'll either become highly stressed, or default on those payments as well. Draw up a realistic budget to help you. What will emerge from that budget are the best ways towards all that reduction of debt – spending less and saving more.

Not spending, spending, spending

Concentrate on the obvious factors first of all – your spending on food, snacks at work, heat and light, dry cleaning bills. Then there are the often-unnoticed haemorrhages of cash – magazines, library fines, mobile phone calls, emergency apologist flower deliveries, etc. Could some forethought reduce spending? Could you read, request or borrow more books at your local library, or set up a magazine swap locally?

Next the larger, and more painful, issues. Is your home too large and expensive to maintain on your own? Is it still a family home for your children? Is it a valuable part of your capital – should you lease it, rather than think seriously of selling it? Would you be financially better off renting somewhere for a few months, or should you sell, invest some proceeds and take out a mortgage? Any advice on the subject will have to take into account the fact that moving would be an extra stress in your life – but if you are under considerable financial stress due to your changed circumstances, some lateral thinking may be called for.

The same could apply to your car. Is it now too large and expensive for your needs? Should you let it go? If you are thinking about a new or second hand car, think your needs through. What size of car do you really need? Do you use it for business, e.g. transporting equipment for catering, or flowers? Do you have dogs to consider? What about tax and insurance payments for large cars? Do you use it to travel widely, on motorways, or for local community commuting? If you opt for a second hand or foreign make, will you be able to get spare parts easily?

TOO MUCH MONTH AT THE END OF THE MONEY?

Pamela Poor	Robin Rich
Has always rented property in a top area, no matter what the property scene – she loves the address. When she did decide to buy, she over-borrowed, thus risking negative equity.	Has always bought properties in her price range, and sold at a profit to move *into* her area. Always chooses a longer mortgage with least borrowing necessary.
Always automatically left savings in building society/ savings account, and never checked the interest rate.	Has always monitored interest rates and returns and switches accounts regularly.
Has no emergency funds, and has often had to pull savings ahead of the due date, incurring penalties.	Put what she didn't need into long term savings with tax efficiency. Always has easy access to savings.
Never manages to have her tax matters ready by the deadline and always incurs penalties.	Does her tax each month and sends her accountant her details on time.

Pamela Poor	Robin Rich
Loves windfalls and spends, spends, spends.	Pops windfalls into tax-efficient accounts and spends the interest.
Upon receiving an inheritance, decided to be sensible and invested in gamble ventures on the markets.	Used her inheritance to reduce her mortgage.
Loves expensive clothes and sales. Shops frequently.	Loves expensive clothes and regularly visits designer sales and discount stores. Is an invited customer to pre-sale days in her top stores.
Holidays at the last minute, often at peak times, in popular resorts.	Picks seasonal borderlines, in less fashionable resorts, but opts for luxury hotels.
Always pays full price for everything.	Uses discount/own brand items for food, basics, etc. Has learned from American friends to ask for cash discount.
Always chooses a new car, with the latest expensive extras, in this season's colours, which reduces re-sale value.	Always chooses a nearly new car, one to two years old, in a standard colour. She maintains it to that standard and keeps the logbook up to date.
Invariably has too much month left at the end of the money.	Never has too much money left at the end of the month, but usually avoids serious debt.

FINANCIAL SAFETY FIRST

1. **Read all documents thoroughly.** Don't be embarrassed to ask questions – many times, if necessary, or to ask for fuller explanations. This especially applies if you are faced with a deal, offer or contract which appears to be too good to be true. If so, it probably is too good to be true – so beware!

2. **Never give total financial control to anyone else – including your partner.** This is even more important in the case of someone who isn't a professional money manager. Never make the mistake of assuming that your partner can automatically handle your finances better than you could, given the correct understanding, support and advice.

3. **Never be pressurised into hasty decisions.** Reputable financial institutions give their clients adequate time to consider the full consequences of actions – including tax and legal implications.

4. **Learn the financial terminology.** There are some excellent guides around, plus well-written financial pages in all the papers. Money management may never fascinate you, but you will understand the basics of what is being discussed. Obviously, this will in turn show that you have some grasp of financial matters, and will also lessen the risk of patronising mis-communication.

5. **Always ensure that you have adequate cover – insurance for your health, home and possessions and pension cover or arrangement for your old age.** Ensure that such cover has been maintained after a death or divorce, and check that it matches rising costs and the cost of replacing new for old. Ensure that you understand (ask questions if necessary) the small print explaining what is covered, and under

what circumstances, e.g. lengthy absence from home, policy requirements may not be met.

Contact

Fiona Price & Partners Ltd, 33 Great Queen Street, Covent Garden WC2 B5AA, Tel. 207 430 0366

CHAPTER FOUR: DIVORCE

Ninety per cent of women say, "I want an amicable divorce – with as little rowing and friction as possible." Men say, "How much is this going to cost me?" – according to top media divorce solicitor Vanessa Lloyd Platt. With such differing attitudes towards divorce and its financial fallout, experts and sympathetic advice is vital.

GROUNDS FOR DIVORCE IN THE UNITED KINGDOM

Divorces are granted following the irretrievable breakdown of the marriage, and the relevant grounds are:

+ **Adultery**: these days, the other party, or the person, who used to be named as the co-respondent, is usually not named.

+ **Unreasonable behaviour**: this is subjective, and can range from violence, neglect and drunkenness to sexual perversions and perceived neglect.

+ **Desertion**: two years uninterrupted desertion is required.

+ **Living apart**: for two years, plus consent.

+ **Living apart**: for five years.

There are also proposals to change Part Two of the Family Law Act with regard to grounds, so be aware of future changes in requirements.

WHAT CAN YOU EXPECT NOW?

According to Simon Bennett, who worked with top London firm Mischon de la Reya, which has handled

Royal and show-biz divorces, "a women has to start to develop a different way of looking at things. Women tend to be careful with money, and avoid debt. But men ride easily with credit outstanding. Also, a woman has to understand that it will take a little time to make money. So, for the first month or so, there may be a financial struggle. The bank account may be cleaned out, so a loan may be necessary. You have to get into a different frame of mind. But hang in there! The loan will be paid from the settlement. Don't worry about the bill – many women do – but each action will help." Simon informs clients about the fee scale from the start, and this is something you should request and understand, especially if you have any lingering doubts.

At the first meeting, Simon likes to persuade his clients to relax, and to start to take care of themselves, even pamper themselves with beauty treatments, outings and small indulgences. This is partly to restore their self-esteem, and partly to prepare them for the task ahead.

The first thing that a woman should do, he feels, is to get details of her husband's assets. In the past, some clients even resorted to searching in briefcases. A full picture of assets and liabilities must be prepared before any decisions can be made.

Both Simon and Vanessa feel that it's vital for a woman to go to a solicitor who specialises in the area – a member of the Solicitor Family Law Association at least. Vanessa feels that a solicitor who is also a trained mediator is a good idea – that way you have a legal representative who is skilled in communication *and* up to date on "the minefield of change" that is divorce law these days.

Should you choose a woman lawyer? According to Vanessa, women "pick up on emotional signals". This can be supportive, as one client told her, "male solicitors tell you facts. I'm interested in someone who's also interested in how I feel." Of course, women solicitors can also pick up on body language and attitudes, which sends out messages about which the client may herself be unaware. This can result in some straight talking. For example – an astute lawyer may draw inferences from a woman's behaviour and attitudes – sometimes a lack of concern about long-term prospects may be linked to the fact that a new man is already in the picture. If a woman falteringly asks what her soon-to-be-ex husband means when he says that he "wants some space", she may be frankly told that he wants to say goodbye, but lacks the courage.

It's unlikely that a good solicitor, of either sex, will become emotionally over-involved with a client. Vanessa feels that if a client needs too much support or wants to talk about her feelings too much, a recommendation to a good counsellor may be part of the service.

Finding the right solicitor for you

Overall, it seems to be an issue of personality compatibility, rather than a question of which sex to choose. Many male solicitors are sympathetic, caring and good communicators, whilst some women find their female counterparts to be vaguely feminist and disparaging of lesser achievers than themselves.

It's vital not to enter the process determined to get it over as soon as possible with a view to developing a new life. Cynics might say "well, solicitors would advise that, wouldn't they?" However, it will take time to get a true picture of the financial, social and practical realities. For the sake of your future, in terms of provision and opportunities, don't try to rush through the process – it will take as long as it takes.

Ensuring financial security

You need to be sure that you can protect yourself financially. If your husband owns the family home, have your solicitor check that a caution is registered against the title of the property, to safeguard your rights. You must also ensure that your lawyer can pro-tect your interest. Get as much detail as you can on accounts, including foreign and offshore, stocks and shares, investments in art, etc. If your husband threatens to sell off assets, your solicitor can obtain an injunction under Section 37 of the Matrimonial Causes Act 1973, to prevent him from disposing of assets. If he has already done so, the courts can freeze those assets, worldwide, under a Moreva injunction.

If your husband has debts, discuss your position with your lawyer. Debts run up will be taken into account in the final settlement. Be aware that if you have a joint mortgage, you are *both* responsible for the full amount. Even if the house has been re-possessed, you may still be chased for any money owed for up to twelve years afterwards. If there is credit card debt, the address rather than the person who lives there, may be a factor, and you could be pursued for your husband's debts. Even if you are not, the mere fact of unpaid debts may affect your credit rating, something you should talk to your lawyer about.

Mediation

Is mediation a good idea? Divorce lawyers feel that mediation has its place, but that there can be a dan-ger of naivety. It's important to have someone in your corner – your husband may well do so. Women can fear conflict, but this very fear can produce or wors-en a situation that already contains dispute. Be aware that a mediator is really only a referee, a ring-master, and will *not* be on your side – it's not a ques-tion of taking sides, if or when things start to get tough for one participant.

Beware of any hidden agendas in contact with your soon-to-be-ex husband. If or when a husband finds that he is not going to get his own way in the due process of events, he may well apply with threats or charm to change your mind. Emotionally confused women have been known to fall for the "you're my best friend", or "why can't we work through this together, after all we've already experienced together in our lives?" routines. Unsure, unhappy and worried about the future, they may further complicate things by meeting their partners, and agreeing – or quarrelling – over matters best decided by more objective judgements. Of course, threats can also be used as tactical manoeuvres. Fear over future settlements, the children's welfare, or decisions over the future of the family home can all terrify already vulnerable women. Even if no hidden agenda is involved, lawyers usually advise clients to stay clear during the stages in which agreements are being hammered out.

Taking advice

Vanessa Lloyd Platt also counsels against listening to friends. "Many may mean well, but some can be ill-informed, and just confuse and worry you." Also, occasionally, some friends may try to live through you, in terms of working out their own agenda over marital conflict or breakdown. So, it's best not to listen – ask your lawyer any relevant questions, and avoid old ex-wives tales.

When should a woman see a barrister? Beware the expensive dangers of seeking counsel too early. There really isn't much point before there has been sufficient financial disclosure. The ideal time, according to Vanessa, is after all schedules questionnaires and requests for information have been dealt with, but "before the FDR hearing". This will be followed, in due course, by the final hearing.

Settlement

These days, settlements are reached by working out the wife's needs and essential requirements and balancing them against available resources, rather than by using any set calculation or percentages. Settlements also reflect the standard of living enjoyed by the couple.

Factors which will be taken into account include the wife's career, or the extent to which she worked, or could return to work. Possible re-training may also be a factor. However, if the woman is older, or was a dedicated homemaker, that would be taken into account. Settlement lengths can vary. Clearly, the length of the marriage is important, as well as the assets brought to it by each of the couple. If there are no children involved, and the woman is younger, with work experience, a settlement might be made for a few years, which would allow re-training, and would then tail off as she became self-supporting. In the case of an older woman who had always worked in the home, and supported her husband in that sense, the deal would reflect her need for security and her inability to produce an income.

In general, solicitors tend to prefer a capital settlement, rather than deal with the possible uncertainties of the "cheque in the post" syndrome, which can sometimes accompany maintenance payments. Of course, money may be tied up, e.g. in a farm or business. Or there may be a situation of low income, but considerable assets. In other cases, it may be possible to capitalise, as there may not be enough assets, or splitting them could result in financial loss. Here, maintenance with capital might be the better choice. If, however, there is a low income, a large capital order might be made, instead of maintenance.

Women should be aware that there are now powers to backdate maintenance payments which have not been index-linked, and which have thus resulted in considerable hardship.

Sometimes, final distributions may have to be postponed. Many solicitors will argue that after the children, a secure home for the wife is vital. There may not be enough capital to buy two homes, so, if children are involved, the final division may be left until the children are eighteen. In order to provide a home for the wife, the capital may be divided, to provide one home, plus a deposit for a second home for the husband. It is not vital to accept the first offer made by an ex-spouse. However, lawyers advise that it is best to be realistic. It also pays to be aware that long, drawn out wrangling will also increase legal costs.

For most women, the pension arrangements will form a vitally important part of the settlement agreement. Following 1996 legislative changes, it is now possible as of right for a woman to claim a share of her husband's pension. This is *not* the same as pension splitting, in which the fund would be divided, and which would provide severance of the fund right now. Rather, this is "ear-marking" an amount, perhaps one-third, to be set aside for her. She will, however, have no influence over his retirement – and, of course, any payments will cease with his death. If he retires at 65, and dies at 66 – that's life – and death. Also it should be remembered that income from pension funds is taxable, whilst maintenance payments are tax-free. From 1 December 2000, for every petition issued after that date a wife or husband will be able to apply for a pension sharing (splitting arrangement) on divorce itself. This is is one of the most far reaching changes in English law for some considerable time. Watch out for fallout from the White-v-White case.

Capital Gains Tax

It's vital also to be aware of the tax implications of the divorce, especially with regard to Capital Gains Tax (CGT). CGT is not payable on the disposal of gifts, which were made between spouses, nor is it payable on your own home or during the first year after a marital breakdown/separation. However, if you dispose of gifts, such as art, jewellery, cars etc.

after that, your liability goes back to the gain made from the first acquisition – not just when you received the gift.

For example – if your husband bought a painting, and after five years, gave it to you when you were married, no CGT would be payable. However, after your "tax free year" following your marital breakdown, if you dispose of the gift for cash, you will have to pay CGT not only on the time since you received the gift, but right back to your husband's original purchase. So, if you have any valuable gifts to sell off to raise money – bear this in mind. There's no need to panic over CGT, however; there is a tax-free threshold for annual disposals, so if you sell off slowly, you're still safe, and indexation is also taken into account.

All of this makes it imperative that you ensure that your decree absolute is not applied for until all the settlement arrangements, pension rights, tax and CGT implications are in order. This is, of course, part of the reasoning behind legal advice to wait, and not rush through to the new life that you now want to start.

Making a will

You will now have to make a new will, At the very least, making a tax efficient will helps to minimise inheritance tax – and will also ensure that your possessions go where you wish, rather than by due course of law. With regard to the will of your ex-husband, in some circumstances, you could claim under the Inheritance Act if you felt that not enough provision had been made for you out of the original estate and you are still dependent on maintenance. A skilled lawyer will put together a settlement, which will reflect this. It's also worth remembering that in general terms, when it comes to former partnerships, a man has some responsibility towards his former wife whilst she is a dependent.

You should also arrange to get power of attorney, and to nominate two people to hold it in case you are incapacitated due to unforeseen circumstances, e.g. illness or accident. Some people opt for family members, some choose girl friends, others include a solicitor. Also arrange for someone to oversee your children's interests and/or education, in case of your death.

Facing the future

These are, of course, just the cold, legal facts of the process. They have to be matched up with a wide range of emotions, even in amicable divorces. These emotions can range from anger and bitterness through to guilt and conscience pangs. Cynics claim that guilt appears when you regret what you've done, whilst conscience displays your fear of future guilt over what you are about to do.

However, the depth of feeling can, of course, have an effect on the expectation and even procedure of the divorce. "Revenge" demands in settlements are well known to lawyers, sometimes in understandable bitterness for perceived penalisation as a home-maker. If a woman feels that she is expected to get a job, even part-time, or is unhappy with her provisions, it will take even longer for her to come to terms with her new life and circumstances. If a woman, has run a home, looked after children and developed a career as well, she may be angry to discover that she is expected to largely provide for her own future, especially if she feels exhausted and over-worked in any case. It's easy to see why good lawyers foster the right attitude along with the right settlement.

Vanessa reminds clients that they can use their obvious staying power to build new lives. That staying power has been used by their men as well – "he needs energy from a whipping boy, and that's what some women have been". They need to develop a sense of self-worth, as their identity has often gone. Yet their staying power, previously used just to cope with life, can push them forward.

Understanding what went wrong

Vanessa also stresses the importance of women acknowledging that they had a part to play in the breakdown, rather than simply blaming their ex-partners. Not only does this help them to move on with their lies, but also to help with any future relationships.

So what, in Simon and Vanessa's experience, are the commonest reasons for divorce? High on any list comes *adultery*. There can be an entire range of reasons cited, from meeting someone younger at work, to the feeling that first wives were nagging. Some men's response to the feeling of being overwhelmed by responsibilities is to have an affair – for fun and escape.

Poor communication is high on any list of causes for marital breakdown, and Simon emphasises this. Simon has also noted regular cases where *work* itself plays a part. Many husbands work long hours, and seem to put their energies and enthusiasm into life outside the home, from wives' viewpoints. Gradual growing apart, with decreasing shared interests can be worsened by physical absence due to long hours, and give increasing silence and lack of concerns in each others' lives. Finally, the wife can come to feel that work is the "other women".

Vanessa also points out that long-term relationships are more difficult to develop as women age. Men their own age are not so attracted. The younger men/older women partnerships are becoming more common, but in Vanessa's experience, these are short lived.

Then there are the practical aspects. A wife, and even an ex-wife, will be provided for when she grows old. A woman on her own, by choice, or after a few relationships, has to accept the dawning realisation that she may *never* be cared for. These observations are not against the philosophy of this book. It is clear that it's not a choice to be taken on a whim, or for fashionable or comparatively trivial reasons. Having said that, for the woman in a truly unhappy marriage who is prepared to deal with *all* the consequences and learn from her experiences – there is the good news that she can create a new and happier life, at any age.

What you need to know from your solicitor:

✦   How long a time frame can I expect this to take?

✦   How much will it cost me – and what can I do to lessen your fees?

✦   Can I stay in my home?

✦   What can I do to protect my share of the assets?

✦   How can I safeguard my children's future – education, inheritance, home etc.?

✦   How can I ensure I have enough to live on – what should I expect?

✦   What about pension arrangements?

✦   Should I go for interim maintenance?

✦   Do I need to take out a loan to cover initial costs?

✦   How will I avoid Capital Gains Tax?

✦   What about debts – his and mine?

✦   What happens to my credit rating?

✦   Will I be able to get a mortgage, with my collateral and income? Will I need to?

✦   What happens if he re-marries, or I do, with regard to wills?

What your solicitor will need to know:

✦ Details of your marriage – time, place, earlier marriages.

✦ Children – dates of birth, education etc.

✦ Assets – yours and his. Get as much detail as you can about bank accounts, shares, policies, funds, trusts, etc.

✦ Debts – yours and his – mortgages, loans, credit cards, hire purchase, business loans.

✦ Your standard of living – use your budget chart to work out an idea. Include all details – from food to car, council tax, pet care, hairdressing bills.

✦ Your work experience – qualifications, career, and professional history.

✦ Your preferences – i.e. to sell the family home, keep it for the children and sell later, lump sum or maintenance etc. Where you would like to live, if you would like to move.

✦ Your plans – further education, return to work, emigration, living with family.

MARRIED OR UNMARRIED BLISS?	
Marriage	*Living Together*
✦ If a shared marriage home is owned by the husband, the wife can to register a caution, registering her right to live there. If the house is bought together, both the wife and husband are held responsible for any debt.	✦ His home or her home. If bought together, both are responsible for the debt.

Marriage	*Living Together*
✦ Without a will the wife is automatically entitled to a share of the estate.	✦ Without a will, a co-habitee is not legally entitled to anything. But if the wife is the mother of his children, she can claim a share for the children if they are dependants.
✦ If they have children, both have rights.	✦ If they have children, she has all rights - he has none. He can acquire them only through the court or by agreement.
✦ A married couple may claim married couple's tax allowance.	✦ Co-habitees may claim single tax allowance only.
✦ If financially able, under legal obligation the spouses must maintain each other, if appropriate.	✦ Co-habitees are under no legal obligation to maintain each other.
✦ Gifts between married couples are exempt from Capital Gains Tax.	✦ Gifts between co-habitees are not exempt from Capital Gains Tax.
✦ Widow of a company pension member may be eligible for life insurance or pension. The wife may be covered under a company health scheme.	✦ Co-habitees do not automatically qualify for insurance or pension. Co-habitees are not usually covered under a company health scheme.
✦ Widows may claim a range of extra state benefits.	✦ Co-habitees may not claim a range of extra state benefits.
✦ Widows benefit from generous inheritance tax relief.	✦ Co-habitees do not benefit from special inheritance tax relief.

Reading

Lloyd Platt, V. (2000) *Secrets of Relationship Success*, (Vermilion, London)

THE SCOTTISH POSITION

Although the grounds for divorce in Scotland have been up till now very similar to those in England, the procedures involved are very different indeed. Those procedures, as well as the law, may be changed in the light of the recent Government White Paper, so we have not produced a step-by-step guide to Scotland at this stage. However, the following points are worth noting:

1. In Scotland, a couple does not have to be married for any particular length of time before a divorce can begin.

2. Adultery can be the basis for an action of divorce no matter how old that adultery is, although a very old adultery may make it difficult to establish that the marriage has broken down irretrievably if the parties have lived together quite happily since then, particularly if the person wishing to raise the action of divorce knew about that adultery and condoned it.

3. Divorce in Scotland proceeds on the basis of an action and not a petition.

4. In Scotland, it is possible to raise an action of divorce on the grounds of two years non-cohabitation with consent, or five years non-cohabitation without consent. These periods are likely to be reduced to one year when the law changes. It is important to remember, however, that the consent must be consent to all parts of the case, including the financial parts because you cannot come back to the court after the end of the case to ask for a capital sum. An action can also be raised on the grounds of unreasonable behaviour or desertion for two years.

5. The legal aid position in Scotland is much more generous that that which applies south of the border.

6. There is no two-stage process in Scotland – once a decree of divorce has been granted, that is that. There is no decree nisi/absolute distinction in Scotland and there never has been.

For clarification of the law in Scotland and for help with your case in particular, it is advisable to contact a solicitor – preferably one who is a specialist family law practitioner. The Law Society of Scotland (tel: 0131 226 7411) can give you details of practitioners in your area.

Source: *Vive Magazine*

DIVORCE IN IRELAND

Divorce in Ireland is governed by the Family Law (Divorce) Act 1996. The court may grant a decree of divorce if it is satisfied that:

1. The husband and wife have lived apart for four of the previous five years.
2. There is no prospect of reconciliation.
3. Proper provision has been or will be made for the spouse and dependent.

Then, if you have a solicitor, he/she must consider the alternatives with you:

✦ the possibility of resolving the difficulties in your marriage

✦ making your own agreement with the help of a mediator

✦ separation by way of agreement in writing

✦ separation by way of a court order

If your spouse does not contest the case, it may take six months or upwards for the divorce to come through, depending on the court lists and the place where the proceedings are issued. If your spouse does contest the case, it could take substantially longer. The Law Society of Ireland can be contacted on tel: 01 672 4800.

Source: *Vive Magazine*

Reading

Mullally, M. (1998) *Law and the Family in Ireland*, (Blackhall Publishing, Dublin)

Wood, K. & O'Shea, P. (1997) *Divorce in Ireland*, (O'Brien Press, Dublin)

CHAPTER FIVE:
WORK

At worst, it pays the bills. At best, it provides interest, motivation, friends, challenges, a social life and new ideas – and it pays the bills. Work is such an important part of our lives today that some studies claim we're closer to our workmates than wider family members. When you're newly alone, or restarting your life, work is vital, as it can bring involvement, stimulation, structure and companionship.

Even over the past fifteen years, the ways we work as well as the careers and jobs we're involved in have changed radically. Part-time, full-time, shared, freelance, consultancy and contract work, skills up dating, re-training, and downsizing – the choices are as bewildering as they are wide-ranging.

Financial problems and perhaps a smaller divorce settlement than anticipated can depress as well as frighten many women about their long-term work prospects. Toss in ageism, family responsibilities and an entire range of networking skills and practices, and many women can find confidence is severely dented.

WORKING PRACTICES

What are your skills, training and work experiences and/or qualifications? Can they be updated? Is promotion a possibility? Will you have to re-train, take a refresher course, or consider a career change?

What would be the preferable option, in view of your financial circumstances? Will your work area be able to support you if necessary, or add to your settlement?

What life experiences – e.g. charity, voluntary, school or community work can you add to your work record in terms of added expertise?

What about family responsibilities? Have you elderly or dependent relatives to care for or about? Can you arrange suitable reliable care? If you have to travel for re-training, how will everyone cope? Do you really need a local job, rather than an ideal job for the present?

If you have to move into a new work area, is there a chance to move into an area you really enjoy? Below are some examples where women have managed to successfully realise a dream or at least move into a related area they enjoy.

Jennifer

Jennifer had always wanted to be an actress, but family circumstances, plus an early marriage ended that ambition. After her divorce she took drama classes to develop her social life, and discovered that what she really enjoyed was the excitement of the creative arts in general. She has now made her way, via her recently acquired administrative skills, into the area of arts administration – and spends long and happy working hours in the world she loves.

Amanda

Amanda always wanted to be a vet, but lacked the academic qualifications. However, she has now found great satisfaction as her part-time office work subsidises her poorly paid animal shelter work.

Caroline

Caroline built up a name as a dress designer, subsidised during her marriage. After her divorce, it became clear that she didn't have the business skills or the ability to create her own business from her talent. Yet her taste and mature selling skills, initially as a temporary stand-in at a local boutique, led to a permanent job. She handles window displays, accompanies her boss to some fashion buying occasions and organises regular fashion shows for charity from the shop.

Gilly

Gilly couldn't afford to live out the struggling writer fantasy. She sticks to writing courses, and works for a small publication as an editorial secretary, with plenty of involvement in layout, design and even the occasional review.

It might be a good chance to think through if you would be better off working, or changing your lifestyle to adapt to changed circumstances. Can you afford to work when transport costs, perhaps a car, working wardrobe, lunches and convenience foods, etc. are all added up – does it actually pay you to go to work?

If you would like advice about your options, it might be a wise investment to spend a couple of hours with a career counselling service. Contact your professional associations or a commercial service for ideas on re-training, re-entry, opportunities or career development.

Contact

Jo Ouston, Lwr. Ground Floor, Nelson House, Dolphin Square, London, SW1V 3NY, for Open Course Schedule.

ALTERNATIVE TECHNOLOGIES AND APPROACHES TO WORK

Move: to somewhere smaller or cheaper, and invest any spare cash – pensions, etc.

Change your workstyle: look at what suits your needs and circumstances, rather than settling at once for traditional hours. Could you work part-time, become self-employed with office contracts or agreements, or self-employed at home? Could you job-share, or telework? Such arrangements might help you to travel less, and would require less outlay in office lifestyles – and more time to organise yourself with less stress – and expensive "comfort" shopping and services.

Could you share a house?: or rent out a room – or use a room as an office or even to store furniture?

Could you use barter in your lifestyle?: have you a marketable skill – cooking, computer skills, child-minding, sewing, graphic design, etc. that could be exchanged for an expensive service, normally paid for by cash? Look for ways to lessen your outgoings, and hence, income needs.

Could you work in a pub: or at weekends in a shop, or at home as a teleworker to allow you to train and develop skills or qualifications for the job or career you want to develop?

TEN COMMANDMENTS FOR THE WORKPLACE

1. **There is no such thing as a job for life any more.** Workers today are becoming used to contracts, golden handshakes or cuffs, mergers, buy-outs and redundancies as part of the fabric of office life. So, be prepared for uncertainty, no matter what your choices. Security can only be found in your own skills and training.

2. **Training is vital, and needs to be constantly updated**, both in your field, and in general

workplace skills. As one ages, the idea of evening or weekend training sessions can be off-putting through to daunting, but seize every opportunity.

3. ***Develop the so-called "core skills"*** which are transferable to whatever area you might move to. They include *Communication* (public speaking, report writing, speech making, presentation, client liaison), *Financial* (budgeting, costing, value – oriented spending and cost-effectiveness) and *Management* (people skills, and hiring, recruiting, supervising and developing others).

4. ***Look towards smaller companies.*** Experts say that this sector is where future employment growth will occur. Smaller companies can also be flexible and innovative enough to defy current prejudices – with ageism included here.

5. ***Be supportive towards your boss***, in terms of helping him/her and allowing him/her to look good in front of superiors.

6. ***Do the jobs that others demur at***, even if it means working difficult hours, overtime or with less glamorous clients or projects than you'd like. Brownie points literally stand to your credit, and also look good on your C.V.

7. ***Performance review.*** It's wise to ensure that you have one, at regular intervals if not annually. You can discover weaknesses, and keep a useful record for your C.V. as well as employment record in case of disputes.

8. ***Work harder when you're not supervised.*** When the cat's away, only very shortsighted mice will play.

9. ***Don't try to play both ends against the middle.*** Using your boss or a situation/project for
   your own ends against the interest of your
   employers, e.g. ignoring contracts which forbid
   you to work for another employer in a similar
   field is usually discovered, and will be noted by
   all.

10. ***Do your job***, what's expected of you and what's
    needed. Many people who fail promotion are
    shocked and angered to find that in the boss's
    view, the job specification hasn't been met.
    Complaints, evasions, time-off and arriving late
    into work can keep you at the work that you
    apparently hate, with no promotion in sight.

MARKET FORCES

As we know, products that are designed for set nich-
es sell best in the market. When your product is
yourself and your skills, you will have to market
yourself well if you want to sell your services. So,
work out your own marketing plan.

Product

Your skills and experience in, e.g. administrative
work, organisation and communication skills.

Niche

Where you would like to work, e.g. nursing, health
care, conventional or complementary.

Aims

To find work that fits in with your skills, aptitude
and personal circumstances. For example a job, full-
time, in your location, within a ten-mile radius, with

a standard, ideally above-rate salary, with training opportunities and full staff benefits, including health care facilities, canteen and sports facilities.

Time scale

Two years to find ideal job. Work to provide experience – within six months. Training and updating of own skills – within two months.

Action plan

Create a timetable for daily work to find a job. For example, mornings – read papers, work on C.V. write application letters, read relevant books. Afternoon – work on fitness, through walks; and once a week, visit specialist library to read trade and professional journals. Once or twice a week, if possible, go to training sessions to learn/relearn skills.

Prepare area for work – clear a table, attach, by plug/extension lead or cordless phone, relevant connection. Ensure area also has stationery, notebooks to detail daily tasks, papers, and journals, which are filed away daily through press cuttings. Files should include research on potential employers, companies, etc. Regularly visit Jobcentre and Training Centres, and keep in touch with advisors.

Regularly pay half-day visits to nearest city for inspiration on office/work clothes, make-up, haircare, etc.

Tools

Mail – letters of application, plus letters of introduction, requests for work experience and advice. *Networking* – with business and work colleagues, plus friends, bearing in mind that between 70 – 80 per cent of jobs are filled by means other than advertising. *Library* – use for information, research, relevant book loans, computer and Internet use.

Following up of leads – magazine articles, radio programmes, local newspaper items relevant to work interest, no matter how far-fetched the contact might seem at the time.

Networking

Networking is a vital skill, indeed habit, for all job seekers. Unfortunately women all too often don't have the necessary skills – especially when they have been out of the workforce. Also, women don't grow up within the natural framework for networking – such as clubs, associations and college re-unions. And when a woman finds herself alone in life, many of her existing contacts may be in her past.

Networking skills:

✦ Get and keep in touch with old business and school/college friends, for lunch, or an informal coffee – and stick to business, rather than family concerns. Join or re-join any relevant business or professional association groups. Think about joining local trade, business or charity groups, and investigate any women's network groups in your area.

✦ Keep in touch with business/professional colleagues. Send congratulatory or condolence cards. Remember that you'll have to work harder when you're the one who needs contacts, news and mentors.

✦ Why go to all that trouble? Because many of jobs, promotions and vacancies are filled by means other than formal interview following advertisement. People hear – or overhear – details about job vacancies and promotion possibilities. Friends, the grapevine or gossip and speculation can provide opportunity for the well informed. In jobseeking, chance favours the prepared mind.

✦ The grapevine, inside track, etc. give advance warning of who is going where, what opportunities are opening up, and who can make things happen.

✦ Friends and family can suggest, recommend and even introduce seekers to opportunities.

✦ Bosses – ex and current, can choose current or ex-staff to work with them.

✦ Ambitious workers can "grow" a job, from secretarial or administrative into management or executive, sometimes in their area of preference.

Making good use of a hobby

Do you have a spare-time interest that you could earn from as well as enjoy the process? Do you cook, sew, paint, decorate, teach, make or ice cakes, arrange or grow flowers? Are you a good listener? Are you interested in complementary therapies? Perhaps you have a variety of skills, none of which might earn you a living, but could, with a part-time job, provide money, interest and opportunities.

When people talk of turning a hobby or interest into a job, the danger is that customer needs and market requirements can be overtaken by interest in the work itself. There's not much point in making up beautifully presented and decorated cakes if you're in an area convinced that shop-bought is best. Or providing executive catering when parents cry out for homework and supervision supplies for the children. Fresh homemade sandwiches delivered to a factory or school complex might not have the creative requirements of smart little dinners, but they can pay for a few of your own. Breeding dogs can be a passion – but regularly walking and pet sitting for commuters' doggy passions can pay better than improving blood lines.

Everyone knows that self-employment equals years of long hours and hard work, plus endless motivation. Even if you decide that you have a marketable skill, and have discovered a true niche for it – this may not be enough to make money. You have to be realistic about the competition, about costing, about cash-flow, about start-up costs and accountancy costs, plus legal fees. Books can help, and so can training, enterprise and start-your-own business courses. If your idea isn't realistic, depend upon it being shot down in flames at an early stage (hopefully, to re-emerge in more marketable terms).

Yet there's no need to despair. Women *do* have a good record in self-employment, whatever their motivations, and are fast becoming a major force in the small business sector.

Tried and tested tips from those who learned the hard(er) way:

1. ***If you work from home, make sure that you have a professional answering manner and service.*** The phone is the first contact with a service or business. If you have children, only let them answer your business extension if they sound mature enough to be assistants. Childish tones spell "unprofessional" to clients. Also, install a proper answering machine/service, fax, paging systems etc. Otherwise you risk exasperating clients, or appearing amateurish.

2. ***Don't start trading until you have ironed out all the problems.*** If you can't get the suppliers/equipment/expertise in order, the client will wonder what you can possibly do for her.

3. **Get pricing right.** Women are notoriously bad at requesting decent rates for the job, and also at increasing rates as the market allows. Remember, people think that you are as good as your rates announce. No point in pricing yourself out of the market, but your rates must cover your costs, with a margin – and remember, if your prices are too low, far from creating interest, you may lead some clients to conclude that you can't be *that* good if your charges are so low.

4. **Ensure that all the legal and administrative requirements are fully in place, and that you understand them and their requirements.** Are you covered for all sorts of liability? Have you met all the legal requirements for your business? Are you covered if someone sues? Are you better to trade as a sole trader, or do you need to form a limited company?

5. **By all means create a good image, logo and business identity – but spend as little as possible when you're starting up.** Women tend to be more realistic than men when it comes to office furniture, fittings and toys. When it comes to business equipment, cheap can be expensive in the long run, but keep your cash flowing, and costs down by using as much existing furniture, storage, etc. as possible, during start-up.

6. **Get back to clients who leave messages.** Even if it is only a mistaken query, the fact that you bother to reply will not only engender discipline in you, but will create a good impression, with unforeseen possibilities.

7. **Develop your selling skills.** You may have the talent and skill, excellent financial back up, a realistic business plan and motivation enough

to inspire an army – but if you can't sell your product, it's all wasted. Are you reaching the clients you want? How could you attract more? Have you thought about word of mouth, mailshots, local advertising, and local magazine or radio coverage? Are your letters or "cold calls" interesting enough to intrigue but not irritate? One page is generally enough, in terms of information and hard sell, to start with. Do you have a distinctive logo, displayed on your letterheads, compliments slips, cards, invoices etc.? Consult a printer about layout, and decide exactly what items will be practical, as well as memorable. Do you really need several types of sheets of headed notepaper? Could some be guillotined to form compliments slips, thus reducing your order, and giving you added flexibility? How many colours do you need? Could you use an established design, or do you need an original? If you have a chance to meet a potential client to make a sale, be prepared for interruptions. You may have to make your case in a few minutes, so organise your portfolio, with examples of your work etc. Don't waste time trying to sell an idea or service, which a potential client doesn't want. If you can't agree on one you can provide, thank her/him and leave. If no answer is forthcoming do a followup the next day.

8.   ***Ask yourself – would you employ yourself?*** Be honest, and if not, why not?

9.   ***Stay healthy.*** You'll be taking on extra stress, and even with full insurance cover (which, of course, you will have in place!) you need to be, and stay, fit and strong enough to put in the extra effort, time and commitment.

10. ***Remember, even as you endure the occasional twinge, or even pang, about company***

perks enjoyed by colleagues, you're in control, and can enjoy some of those perks – business class travel, top health care, research trips away, in time and when you choose. No one can say that you're too old, out of touch, unemployable – look after it, and your best boss can be yourself.

DO YOU WANT A LITTLE COMPANY?

More often than not, business equals capital – for equipment, leasing, premises, wages, fees, etc. Women generally seem to prefer to start small – kitchen sink drama can have many permutations these days. Women's routes into and motivation towards their own businesses can also be circuitous and original. A hobby or interest might lead to private commissions, and perhaps skills updating. An opportunity in the locality to provide a service might tie-in with demanding home responsibilities and unusual free hours. Inspiration might be enhanced by the desire to provide employment or opportunities for children. Changed personal circumstances might lead to training or a further education course, and onto a small business course, due to apparent unemployability.

The plethora of excellent books, guides and advice on training makes any further information on the basics of setting up a small business redundant. Here instead, are ten tips from those who have learned from their mistakes:

1. **Choosing – and working with – a partner, is like choosing and making a life with a husband or partner – and needs as much care and attention – if not more!** Breaking up may be even harder (and expensive) to do with a business partner. So, make sure that you have compatible aims, skills and beliefs.

2.   **Keep your borrowings as low as possible.**
     Lease or rent, or even beg/borrow rather than
     buy, if possible. Establish whether an agreed
     overdraft might be more economical than
     expensive borrowing or term loans. Could you
     use freelancers, outworkers or rented premises
     when necessary – rather than face the outlay of
     fully rented premises?

3.   **Get to know – and keep in touch with – peo-
     ple in your professional or trade associa-
     tion,** and also join any local groups.

4.   **Make sure that you have good back up at
     home when you start up.** With self-employ-
     ment, you can, if necessary, work late or some-
     how deliver the promised goods, in spite of
     domestic crisis. When financial advisors, bor-
     rowing, costing and maybe staff are involved,
     your entire, undivided attention is needed – for
     many long hours each day.

5.   **Decide the level to which you are prepared
     to take the business realistically.** Everyone
     hears about, and is prepared for failure. But
     what happens when a small business shows
     signs of sudden expansion? It's important for
     you to know from the start what aspects you
     enjoy most – and what skills you can best offer.
     Do you really enjoy the hands-on aspects of the
     work? Do you want to see expansion of your
     ideas? Are you happy to discuss borrowing and
     confer with bankers about future plans, with
     accompanying paperwork? Would you be happy
     to sell out, if the opportunity came? Would you
     consider a franchise scheme? Or would you be
     happier to stay small, but flexible enough to
     meet changing demands?

6.   **Make the most of local and charitable pub-
     licity.** Sponsor charity runs, give hampers and

baskets as raffle prizes, and support local ven-
tures or training. The costs can be minimal
when compared with advertising, and the good
will – and local publicity – will be lasting.

7. ***Take your business-self very seriously.***
When a man is introduced as the whiz kid that
has set up a splendid new service, which can
only go from strength to strength – he usually
nods, and talks about expansion plans. All too
often, a woman merely insists that she's been
lucky really, and it's not *that* big a venture really, and that she has had a lot of help...why? Or
do we need to even ask?

8. ***You will still encounter put-downs, snide
comments and resentment.*** You'll need to
develop the confidence to recognise it as such.

9. ***Don't fall into the trap of assuming that
long hours equal effective work.*** Ensure that
you're working effectively as well as efficiently;
smart as well as hard. And that includes dealing with stress in your life, with regular self-
care.

10. ***One of the benefits of a small business is
that it can be flexible and swift to respond
to changing market demands.*** So make sure
that your finances, staffing and premises allow
you to cut back as well as expand as fast as
possible. Crisis management often leads to
management in crisis.

Reading

Ballback, J. and Slater, J. (1998) *Making Career Transitions*, (Kogan Page, London)

Cartwright, S. and Holmes, T. (1996) *Midlife Career Change, Desire or Necessity?* (Kogan Page, London)

Dakers, H. (1998) *NVQs and How to Get Them,* (Kogan Page, London)

Department of Education, Employment, *Second Chances,* (Lifetime Careers Ltd, Wiltshire)

CHAPTER SIX:
SOCIAL LIFE

Second only to the complexities and challenges of dealing with a new financial way of life, is the task of creating a new social life. This is true at any age, but especially when you're out of your thirties. There are many practical reasons for this. The natural meeting places, such as parties, college life, clubs and associations have largely gone with youth and natural pairing off. A few generations ago, hostesses and country house parties or weekends allowed natural socialising at all ages, but these are now restricted to the very wealthy and influential. Hence, with no reflection on your personal attractions, it may be very challenging to develop a satisfying solo social life, with prospects and opportunities to form further close relationships.

The old adages still hold true – follow your interests, skills, talents and experience, and develop them locally, in your community or in your network. However it must also be said that at some future stage you may miss the shared interests and backgrounds of those you may have met at dinner parties, clubs, charity events, and who formed the "tapestry" of your earlier social life. You may want the company of people whose standards, outlook and world-view you instinctively share. This will take investigation, research, patience and resilience, as well as the willingness to try all sorts of activities and interests. The plus side is that all that practice will make you more confident, relaxed and an even better social mixer.

However, to start off, whether you need a new social life or simply want one, start with your interests and skills. Do you have a special cause, a fascination or natural aptitude? Do you love the countryside,

gardening, or have an interest in dogs or wildlife? Are
you concerned with the elderly, or the handicapped?
Are you a natural organiser, or good at "hands-on"
demands? Are you an efficient fund-raiser, with
connections and contacts to call on? A skilled home-
maker? A good businesswoman?

SOCIAL ENGINEERING

One of the hardest acceptances for any newly single
woman is that the process of developing a social life
is up to her. For many women, the steady dropping
of all those invites on the doormat – corporate entertainment, dinner parties, club dinners, are a fact of
life. Once on your own, however, even if fortunate in
the loyalty of friends, it's up to you. *You* have to
investigate, initiate, suggest, propose, persuade, get
yourself there, greet, talk, invite and maintain any
new relationships you may make – and you have to
keep on doing it over and over again, because if you
don't – nobody will do it for you.

Many women still hate attending receptions, parties, groups, classes and entertainment on their own.
This can be due to vestigial feelings of embarrass-
ment – "what will people think of me, that I couldn't
get a partner?", or simple preference for sharing an
experience with another person. Women who have
come through both these self-induced prejudices
comment that the awful truth is that *no-body* is
interested enough to even give a second thought to
your solo state, and that on your own, you don't have
to deal with the downside of companionship.
Remember those evenings when you were faced with
boredom, anger, resentment, drunkenness, aggres-
sion or superciliousness? You're free of that as well
as of a companion. Also, on your own, you're easier
to approach. You're not so inhibited by the preferences and prejudices of someone with you – and one

person is easier to include if something new or interesting is proposed.

However, no one will pretend that it is easy to be constantly pro-active in terms of keeping in touch, planning, suggesting dates and ideas – and dealing with no-shows and cancellations when you have made plans. The cheerier news is that it does get easier as you go on, and develop a wide network – and the confidence to suggest, try out and follow up on new, enjoyable ideas and projects.

GUEST APPEARANCE

So, on the premise that the easiest way to develop new friendship is to work on our existing acquaintances, some feisty female survivors share their tips:

✦ "The first cocktail party or reception on your own can be horrific when you're used to being a twosome. Just walking in through that door alone is terrifying. If it's a private party, I beg my hostess, in fact snatch from her, any plates or edibles and scoot around with them. You can "work the room", with a safety net – you're bringing people food, so you've a right to interrupt them".

✦ "These days, more and more people are having staff, even if it's only friends' children in uniform, hand round drinks, so I've devised a routine. I walk into the room, pause, and smile at the opposite corner, and stroll across the room, as if I've recognised someone. That gets me into the group, and away from the door. If necessary, I pretend I've mistaken the person beside me. And I've forced myself to scan the room and say 'now, who here will *I* find interesting', rather than worry about what they'll think of me. I'm afraid it's true that people do take you at your own valuation..."

✦   "I head for groups – easier to join than two-
     somes of either sex. I gently edge in from a gap,
     apologise for bumping someone, and just catch
     eye contact when a story is told. Then you're
     included in a laugh, or nod, and you're in..."

✦   "I simply introduce myself – the full formal,
     'How do you do, I'm ...', with a grin to take the
     pomposity off it all...I find that most times, peo-
     ple feel manners-bound to promptly introduce
     themselves, and you're on your way..."

✦   "If I'm invited to a dinner on my own, and there
     is a reception beforehand, I try to mix and min-
     gle, although I do tend to 'cling' to people out of
     panic. When I feel that I've done my stuff – and
     I usually arrive as late as possible for the recep-
     tion, I slip down to the dining room, and find
     my seat. Often, other people come to the table
     early as well, and I smile and introduce myself
     – so I'll know someone to talk to or smile at dur-
     ing the meal..."

CHARITABLE INSTINCTS

Charity work has long been accepted as an excellent
way to give and receive – so whether you want to
help, work for a conviction or cause or create one
yourself, start with your own interests and abilities.
What can you do?

✦   **Organising skills**: put together fundraisers
     from coffee mornings and lunches to outings,
     gardens or stately homes. Bear in mind that top
     organisers warn it's increasingly difficult to
     tempt people to dinners and receptions – we're
     less impressed by names and places these
     days, even for good causes.

✦ **Hands-on skills**: deliveries, physical work, such as clean-ups, restoration.

✦ **Specialist skills**: listening, cookery, design, business, art, etc.

Some people want to take their skills abroad to where they are actually needed. However, be prepared for culture shocks:

✦ "I had the opportunity to go to India for a few weeks with a religious charity – and I felt I couldn't turn it down. It was quite traumatising at first. Charities have to save money, so it was cheap airlines, long bus rides, heat, smells and delays. The centre where we stayed was primitive, but scrupulously clean. But I was worried all the time about my health. I taught English and reading skills, and felt ashamed much of the time – these incredibly poor people were so grateful, and kept giving me gifts. I saw so much – filth, disease – I'm so grateful now for the NHS. It all changed me. I haven't gone all 'holier than thou', but it made me think and reassess what I see as important. I'd like to go to Eastern Europe now, and I think I could help better following my Indian experiences".

Bear in mind that people work for charities for all sorts of reasons – social as well as altruistic, and may want recognition on a grand scale, so tact and diplomacy are called for, especially at high levels. The adage that a camel is a horse designed by a committee was never so true as in this setting. Petty feuds and working styles may complicate matters. Be prepared for the fact that 80 per cent of the work may be done by 20 per cent of the group – including yourself.

MUTTON DIVERSIFYING AS LAMB

Could your developing social circle include younger friends? Never mind your wrinkles, hardening of the attitudes is as ageing as hardening of the arteries. If you're young for your age you:

✦ Could keep au fait with the current music scene – and aren't annoyed when a new group does a cover version of *your* favourite from a quarter of a century ago.

✦ Are computer literate.

✦ Could be up to date with films, books, and turns of phrase and dances.

✦ Could be shocked by some of the younger generation's attitudes, but open minded enough to see the possible benefits, and understand motivations.

✦ Wouldn't dream of not going with a group to a club, or the latest dance spot.

✦ Think that people who take up windsurfing, gliding, young lovers (of either sex), cosmetic surgery or new age philosophies are cool, rather than sad.

✦ Are seen by your grown up family as someone to whom they can talk, rather than Mother, Granny or Aunt.

✦ Don't think that May December relationships of either sex are a bit odd.

✦ Are unconvinced that standards have radically dropped over the past couple of decades.

✦ Know that *these* are the Good Old Days in the making.

✦ Don't feel that the best years of your life are well and truly over.

HAVE A GREAT WEEKEND

Few phrases dampen the spirits of the newly and perhaps unwillingly alone more than the well-meant and apparently universal hope for the pleasures of the weekend. Feelings of exclusion, nostalgia, hurt and even despair can add to existing loneliness, and ironically may even be made worse by observing other people's togetherness. We all know that for singles, advance planning for weekends is vital – but what if the unthinkable happens? It's a long weekend and your companion phones on Friday night to cancel. Two or three days of isolation loom. What to do?

✦ If a foreign break away, trip to a concert or outing has been booked and paid for; go anyway, on your own. At that stage cancellation charges would be so high, that you might as well enjoy yourself. Don't be put off by the idea of travelling alone. If you're nervous, tell the relevant staff, and you will certainly be especially well looked after, and have a wonderful experience.

✦ Read your local or national paper for seminars, meetings, groups or gatherings in your area, and check if there are places available. Lots of people go alone, and you'll have a chance to try something new and meet people.

✦ Call your friends on the off chance that someone might be free for a visit or a trip – but don't expect them to cancel for your benefit.

✦ Keep a stock of weekend break brochures in your home, and ring a couple to see if they have any last minute vacancies within driving distance.

✦ Decide that you're going to postpone your weekend, and do all the jobs you've been putting off – from filing to cleaning, decorating to DIY.

Along with your supplies, bring home a video or book with which to reward yourself.

✦ Decide to create your own health farm experience at home. Set the scene by a brief clean and tidy up, and buy some fresh flowers. Change the sheets on your bed, and prepare a thoroughly relaxing and sensual experience. Buy in some salads and cooked foods – cut down on cooking. Use up all those beauty products, and deep-cleanse, condition, oil and polish yourself to relaxed bliss.

HOLIDAYS

Re-think the whole idea if you feel self-conscious or forlorn as a solo traveller. Look for *specialised holidays*. Ideally, they will reflect your interests, but if you're adventurous, you can get involved with anything from painting to riding or gardening. There is often a shared booking arrangement in any case, to keep costs down, with plenty of singles around, so you won't feel isolated.

If you feel unwilling to take on the challenge of solo travelling in a large hotel (or the finances involved), why not opt for a series of top of the range *bed and breakfast* accommodations? Remember, these days, it may only be the size and room numbers which down grade them from exceedingly comfortable hotels. Choose several *short breaks*, ideally abroad, rather than the more conventional fortnight's break, if you feel that you couldn't cope with your own company for that time.

Why not go on an *educational holiday*? Learn to play bridge, speak another language, cook, fish, sail, take photographs, sing – the list is endless, the surroundings often beautiful and the social opportunities often excellent.

If a holiday for you remains firmly linked to the presence of familiar faces, look into the possibilities of creating your own *house-party* with friends, perhaps for a long weekend, at a small hotel, which takes block bookings? Why not rent a listed building, folly or castle for a special celebration or reunion. Americans do it all the time – organising annual get-togethers as a regular social event. If you could afford it, why not look into the rental of a winter sport chalet, or a continental villa, to be shared with a few friends who could afford it as part of a group, but not alone? Insist on financial deadlines for deposits, and build in safeguards against no-shows or dropouts.

MATCHMAKER, MATCHMAKER...

The overview of relationships has changed utterly over the past decades, and men and women now have entirely different expectations from relationships a generation ago. Gone are the days when a marriage provided security, financial support, social compatibility and housekeeping skills between the partners. Now, the skills required include (ideally, anyway) emotional sensitivity, friendship, sharing of responsibilities and great sex. Increasingly, men say that what they want in a relationship is good sex with a loving friend, whilst women expect much more than a combination of provider, odd-job man and social partner.

If you want a relationship, it may be necessary to change your standards. Now, before you start to wonder if it's still acceptable to require a partner with his own body parts intact on your private "must have" list, what we're really talking about is flexibility over eligibility. Would you consider someone less physically appealing than previous partners? Someone less financially secure? Someone from a different race or background? A younger man? How much younger?

Would you consider a part-time relationship? A relationship that wasn't going to lead to marriage?

All relationships have baggage – children, financial problems, ex-wives or partners or personal problems. But just how much baggage are you prepared to accept? Sexual or emotional problems or preferences? Addictions? Lack of commitment?

Once you've established just what you're looking for, e.g. a live-in relationship, a committed marriage, or a relaxed, fun, open-ended affair, you can think about where you could meet such a partner. Here again, the most successful matches can come from interests, interests and interests. A few examples of over-fifty pairings:

✦   A backpacking trip.

✦   An open day for the governing body of a professional organisation.

✦   An antique fair.

✦   A music festival.

✦   A wine course.

✦   A health farm.

And then there's the marriage bureau. Opinion is sharply divided on the subject of dating agencies and bureaux. For many, they're sensible and modern versions of family introduction networks, and weed out unsuitable candidates – if you choose your agency wisely. For others, they represent a sad – and maybe dangerous acceptance of defeat. What people don't always recount is how exposed and vulnerable they feel whilst diplomatically being informed of their market suitability – and depression at being faced with suitable   matches!   It   helps   to   be   honest about your motives. Can you take the rejections, or would searching for a wider social circle be better? Or would the fee be money well spent, rather than wasted on fruitless local socialising? Ask *lots* of questions from any agency – get details of such questions from:

Society of Marriage Bureaux, 18 Thayer Street, London W1M 5LD

Single Again, Suite 33, 10 Barley Mow Passage, London W4 4PH, Tel. 0193 8561 308

WHEN SALLY MET HARRY	
When Sally met Harry through a dating agency...	*When Sally met Harry through friends...*
Sally met: ✦ *Alan*, who lied about his age, height, job and interests ✦ *Nigel*, who expected a one-night-stand ✦ *Charles*, who was devoted to his elderly mother, but wanted a nurse for future years ✦ *Peter*, who was a bitter divorcee ✦ *Chris*, who was a dirty old man ✦ *Tom*, who was a dirty old married man ✦ *Harry*, who is possible friendship material, but nothing more.	Sally met: ✦ *Carol*, on a weekend course and was introduced to... ✦ *Jenny and Tom*, who invited her to a concert where she met... ✦ *Kate*, who after a lunch date took her to a gallery owned by *Mark and Peter* from whom she bought a print by... ✦ *Alastair*, whom she met at a viewing and who invited her to a brunch where she met his father... ✦ *Mark*, who had a cousin... *Harry*, who asked Sally out for dinner, which developed into a friendship, which developed into...

SOCIAL MOBILITY

When you do meet someone, bear in mind the new, younger generation's rules:

1. Get into shape for love – like you would for any interesting adventure. Know what you want – and don't settle for less. Get your life into shape – before you put love into it. Remember the old adage – men choose someone who fits in with what they want to be – women pick out the person they *want* to be.

2. Don't invest all your emotional energies too soon, i.e. after sex, or a little gentle speculation from concerned and loving friends. The old ideas of courtship and suitability had some merit.

3. Learn from men – and be confident in your approaches, outlook and failures as well as successes. Men often blame the circumstances, whilst women blame themselves.

4. Don't be *too* nice, reliable or available. Familiarity doesn't always breed content, and sadly, if you don't blow your own trumpet – no – one may think it worth the effort.

5. Keep the relationship in perspective – alongside friends, colleagues, loved ones and work. And if it's not working out – let it go and move on to something – or someone – better. Learn from your mistakes, or lessons, and learn to see them as experience.

SEMI-DETACHED STYLE

One of the advantages of singledom is the chance to create relationships which meet the needs of all concerned. If there is no social or ethical need to conform to society's norms for relationships, e.g. to raise a family, then could you create a relationship, which meets your needs and creates optimum happiness from what *is* available to you?

Clive and Jenny

Both in their 60s, Jenny and Clive enjoy separate lives, together. Wary after previous marriages, they valued freedom, but also emotional closeness. So, when their relationship became serious, they agreed to stay in their own homes, 20 miles apart. They visit each other regularly, with stay-overs. Jenny is happy not to have to cook and clean for Clive, whilst he is happy not to worry about her finances or DIY. They take holidays together, hill-walk, go antiquing and attend courses. Both joke that they are too set in their ways to marry, but care for each other deeply and want to keep it that way. Hence they resolutely ignore hints from friends and family, who want to neaten their lives.

Susan and Tim

Susan and Tim are 50-plusses, who were both previously married. Tim has teenage children who often stay with him. Susan grew up with a stepfather and decided never to put a child through the misery she endured, at any age. She refused to consider living with Tim, but sold her old home and bought a flat within walking distance of his. They pop in and out virtually on a daily basis, stay over and eat together when he is alone. Susan has gradually been accepted as a presence in Tim's life, but in the knowledge that she will not replace their mother. Susan finds plenty to do at weekends and holidays when they are around. She isn't lonely or bitter, but happy, as she knows that she is the only woman in Tim's life.

Teri and Jo

Teri and Jo also have separate lives – on separate continents. Both wealthy, they met in North America on an educational course. Teri spends about two months each year with Jo in the US, which is home to Jo, but sometimes Jo comes over to the UK, home to Teri. They are both extremely free-spirited and love travelling together, and have recently considered a three-month round-the-world cruise. Both have very full, independent lives, and rather unusually, have no wish to know about other relationships – other than precautions against infections. They both see fidelity as non-essential, but as a compliment, and instead prefer to focus on shared interest and fun.

Susan and Mark

Susan and Mark have a companionate relationship. They met at a health farm, where Mark, now in his 70s, told her that he was devoted to the memory of his late wife. As the relationship progressed, he made it clear that his estate would go to his children, and that companionship was all he could offer. Susan in her late 50s, lonely and alone, wanted just that. A brief physical relationship wasn't a success – to Mark's disappointment, and to Susan's relief, as she did not find him physically attractive. However, as close partners and friends they attended concerts, theatre and parties. Her life has opened up, much to the astonishment of both herself and her friends.

Laura and Neil

Laura and Neil's relationship, the classic pairing of the older woman and the younger man, causes much gossip in their small village. After her divorce, Laura re-invented herself as a fit and glamorous woman, and took a job as a manager of a small antiques shop. At her desk in the large window, electrician

Neil spotted her. Friends were initially incredulous at the 25 year age gap, as well as differences in education, interests and social background. Her friends secretly envied her, but prophesised that it would all end in tears, which it did after a few months. However, Laura has no regrets. She feels that unlike her marriage, she experienced real love, and has been left with no bitterness. She feels that she hasn't missed out on passion, and has been boosted by the interest of such a young man. In her view, even if Neil were her last love, it would be an ideal way to bow out,

Reading

Floodlight, Yellow Pages (associations and charities), BT directory, local guidebooks, festival guides, specialist magazines (course/associations).

Contact

300 Group, (to increase women M.P.'s) Horsham, West Sussex, Tel. 01403 733 797

Arvon Foundation (writing courses, Yorks, Devon, Scotland) Totleigh Barton, Sheepwash, Beaworthy, Devon EX21 5NS, Tel. 01409 231 338

British Trust for Conservation Volunteers, 36 St Mary Street, Wallingford, Oxon OX10 OEU, Tel. 01491 839766

Council for Protection of Rural England, 25 Buckingham Palace Road, London SW1W OPP, Tel. 020 7979 6433

English Heritage, Fortress House, 23 Savile Row, London W1X 1AB, Tel. 207 973 3000

National Trust, (Membership) P.O. Box 39, Bromley, Kent BR1 3BR, Tel. 0208 3151111. (working holidays) P.O. Box 84, Cirencester, Glos GL7 1ZP

Skyros, (personal development holidays in Greece) 92 Prince of Wales Terrace, London NW5 3NE

The Pudding Club, (meets twice monthly to enjoy superb dinner, with pudding). Chocoholics, (weekends of eating, treasure hunting and factory visiting chocolate!) both at Three Ways House, Mickleton, Chipping Camden, Glos. GL55 6SB, Tel. 01386 438 429

The Wildlife Trust, The Kiln, Mather Road, Newark, Notts. NG24 1WT, Tel. 01636 677711

Wine Society, Tel. 0143 874 1177

Women's Royal Voluntary Service, Milton Hill Hse, Abingdon, Oxon, Tel. 01235 442 9000

CHALLENGING TIMES

Maybe what's really needed is a stimulating (and perhaps moderately risky) challenge to stir the blood, and give you back that twinkle in your eye – even if it does spring from initial fear:

✦ **Start up a Share Club**: pool your surplus cash with friends (three to twenty) and buy shares. Then, with an agreed minimum amount (around £1,000 is recommended), you buy shares, according to established guidelines, and with agreed monthly contributions from each member, continue to expand your portfolio. Thanks to clear guidelines, the club is simple to run, and no previous share-dealing experience is necessary. In fact, some of the most successful groups say that they joined as much as for the regular meetings – usually once each month, as for the chance to learn about stocks and shares and make money. Each member is usually involved in an area to research, e.g. business, retail sectors, or the media. Members can become skilled – and earn whilst they learn.

Contact

Get details, and buy the start-up manual from Proshare, Investment Clubs, Centurion House, 24 Monument Street, London EC3R 8AQ, Tel. 207 2201730.

✦ **Organise a re-union:** of school friends, college chums or even people with whom you used to be friends. Use library facilities, college/university/past pupil associations or company addresses to contact them. Persistence is vital, as is the ability to co-ordinate and arrange a suitable time and place. Start with a lunch date – in case you find you have nothing in common but old grudges.

✦ **Train for and run a marathon:** it will take at least several months and perhaps as long as a year to get into shape. You'll have to put in hours of slow build-up practice. It *does* help to train with friends, or even to get supervision from a gym. When it comes to the race, this is one time where it really is the taking part that counts – that's what you remember. There is also the added bonus of friendship – you might even find yourself staying with new friends in various capitals as you get involved in the international marathons.

✦ **Set yourself a physical challenge:** it could be a trip on an Outward Bound course – several are tailor-made for women. Or it could be a challenge such as coping with a long held fear – of water or heights. Why not learn to swim, dive or abseil? It could become a luxurious experience – such as a trip in a hot-air balloon, or in a glider – what it is doesn't matter, so long as it stretches you, and gives you a feeling of pride and achievement. Nor need it be a matter of dealing with fear. You might decide to go on a camping or walking holiday at home if you're normally a hearth-bound creature. Or you might, after some training, decide to take a walking or hiking trip to an unspoilt country – if you're the type who normally likes to view such places from the comfort of a five star hotel.

✦ *If you have a personal or community interest, why not learn how to self-publish* with some of the excellent books on desktop publishing? It's now possible to create a wide range of newsletters, books, guides, local histories and even personal recollections or thoughts, for permanent record. When you become involved, it's also a great way to meet a wide range of people, as you research and interview for your work.

✦ *Feel unappreciated or even redundant in your homemaker role?* If you always enjoyed cooking or childcare, why not develop that ability to open up your life, travel or even start a new career? The Au Pair and Nanny's Guide to Working Abroad, from Vacation Work Publications, covers training and provides a guide to agencies and expectations in 22 world-wide countries. If you're a good cook, the world is your palate, from ritzy motor racing catering to discreet country house and shooting parties. The Good Cook's Guide to Working Abroad, also from Vacation Work, covers training courses, finding a job, specialised areas, business issues and masses of useful advise and ideas.

✦ *If you modelled when you were younger*: either for photographic or catwalk work, bear in mind that there is a small but expanding market niche for older women models – magazine, catalogue, advertisement work etc. Agencies that work with mature models report increasing applications from hopefuls. Remember, however, competition is just as tough, if not more so, than it was thirty years ago.

✦ ***The Gap Year is no longer the province of the young***: Career break, life–change and retirement options mean that people of all ages want to become involved in volunteer work at home or abroad, for long and short periods. Teachers, doctors, nurses, business experts and other specialists are all needed. Could your skills be used? At home, could you volunteer for an organisation like the Winged Fellowship, which provides respite for careers, and holidays for those with disabilities?

✦ ***Make a contribution in your community***: Schools need enthusiastic and able governors to take responsibility for budgets, and to ensure the school provides the best possible education. If you care about the next generation, and are prepared to operate as part of a team and are open to new ideas, then ask at your local library, or read the DEE leaflet. Or could you be a magistrate? Write to the Lord Chancellor Department for details.

Contact

Lord Chancellor Department, Selbourne House, 54-60 Victoria Street, London SWIE 6QW.

✦ ***If you love children***, and are truly open-minded, adaptable, tolerant, accepting and patient, could you become a foster carer? These days, single people are acceptable, as are those living with a partner, and maturity is a plus. You also need to have experience with children – as a mother or a nurse or child-minder for example, and to have time, energy and good health.

Contact

National Foster Care Association, 87 Blackfriars Road, London SE1 8HA, Tel. 207 620 6400.

✦ *If you sigh for those weekends away, but are on a restricted income, think about house-sitting*: accommodation can be luxurious, but bear in mind that you are responsible for the house's security – many agencies don't allow absences of longer than three hours, and insist on overnights. This is one area in which maturity is a must, rather than an ideal – absolute reliability and excellent references are required.

✦ *If you have experience, ideally professional, with animals, consider pet sitting*: however, this can be fairly demanding – detailed dietary requirements, walks, grooming and constant attention will be required – worse than children, say some participants.

Contact

Animal Aunts, Tel 01730 821529

✦ *Would you be prepared to swap your home for the holidays?* Many enthusiasts see the fact that they are in yours, and you are in theirs as a guarantee – as well as the means to a cheap holiday in a foreign spot. The Internet is a good source.

Contact

HomeLink International, Tel. 01344 842642, Rep of Ireland, Tel. 846 2598, Intervac International Home Exchange, Tel. 01225 892208

✦ *Change your life from choice – as well as necessity*: rather than resisting changes in your life – home, family members, finances, etc., decide to take control over your *own* life from scratch. Work out what *really* matters to you, and develop your home, work and friends to fit your style of change, rather than feeling forced into unwilling change, inch by inch.

✦ **Experience some fun**, if not fortune and fame, and appear on television or in a film. Write to the audience participation, quiz or game shows, reply to one of the chat shows or just request tickets to a show you enjoy. Some people have developed hobbies, if not a taste for fame, out of regular "guest" appearances – and if you become known as a "rent-a-mouth", you'll even be asked along to some, even though you may be "planted" to ask questions, or put forward a controversial viewpoint. When it comes to the big screen, even if you don't want to become a seriously committed extra, there are still ways to join in. Keep an eye on advertisements in local papers, read the relevant publications such as The Stage or Screen International, which gives location details. It's important to realise that the pay won't be much, you'll hang around for long hours, and possibly get cold and wet in unbecoming costume. However, the food on location is generally excellent, and whilst stars generally stay ensconced in comfort, it *is* exciting to see a household name en route to scenes in the same production you're involved with. But don't bother to boast until you see the big screen version – you've most likely ended up on the cutting room floor.

✦ **Work towards living out your dream**: whether it's going round the world, flying on Concorde, attending a glittering ball, getting in print, owning a designer dress or learning to play the piano beautifully – research, ask questions, save and plan to make your own dreams come true – by your own efforts. And when you decide to do it, the information, chances, plus ways and means that come your way will amaze you.

✦ **Kick-start the New Year by doing something
utterly out of character**: learn to drive, shoot,
surf the net, flirt, cut your hair and/or dye it,
or ask an attractive man out on a date. All
right, if you're chicken, get two tickets beforehand. If you're known for your bubbly, jokey
personality, take up a more serious interest or
course than you're used too. Regularly read a
paper with a view utterly opposed to your own;
within the bounds of personal safety, stand up
for your beliefs – protest, campaign for or support a cause which you feel is just and reasonable, even if your family and friends don't agree.

✦ **Let go**: the toughest challenge of all.
Understand that it's not a question of giving in
or up, rather accepting that some fights are no
longer worth the struggle, and that you might
just be continuing to fight after the battle is
over. Whether it's a house, a relationship, a
feud, a prejudice, a job, a role or perceived status, or an unused possession – if it's in your
way, holding your attention and energy, taking
space and joy from your life – then let it pass
and move on without bitterness. The rewards of
peace of mind and freed energy will more than
make up for any regrets or sense of loss.

We often admire characters, especially women, from
previous eras for their determination, willpower and
physical endurance. Whilst many had the appear-
ance of frail femininity, which they adeptly preserved,
they were in reality true survivors. Those Edwardian
Grandes Dames really knew how to endure, without
a television talk show or therapist in sight.

Women who lived in earlier times also shared such
spirit. They lived in conditions which we would have
found intolerable – the epidemics, childbirth, expectations and relationships they had to deal with,
demanded certain life skills and attitudes. Abroad,

the Pioneers in new worlds, the Puritans and most of the women who dealt with life that was their lot in the days of building the New Frontier in America and Australia. One quality all had was a hardiness of spirit. It's a phrase that's gone out of fashion these days. Yet the qualities it encompassed could serve us well today...

Hardiness is about:

✦ Surviving and enduring in the face of difficult odds.

✦ Not demanding happiness. Hardy spirits know it's not a right in life, and that often, as American President Lincoln observed, we're about as happy as we make up our minds to be.

✦ Loving nature and understanding the passing of the seasons and stages in life, and that to all things there is a season...which will pass.

✦ Not being afraid of hard work / and being fervently independent, in spirit as well as lifestyle.

✦ Not seeing yourself as a victim, even in cases of tragedy, and taking time to heal before moving on.

✦ Being courageous, and having resilience to keep coming back again and again after disappointments and setbacks.

✦ Adapting to circumstances, loss, success and hurt – without losing a strong sense of self.

✦ Being rooted in your community, and receiving help from friends and family, rather than depending on any state or government help as a right.

✦ Not seeking revenge and/or letting yourself be consumed with bitterness.

✦ Counting on yourself.

BEING YOUR OWN PERSONAL COACH

So, to sum it all up, what better than to get the advice of the new breed of inspirational gurus – the *Personal Coach*. Just how *do* you move on?

Find out what you want to do – three or four things that you want to achieve. Call them goals, aims, projects – decide, and write them down. Brainstorm.

Include them in your life as if you already have them – act as if you have them, or as you would wish to be. Fake it till you make it. Get rid of all the things that stop you from doing what you want to – fears, disapproval, procrastination, etc.

Clear your life – to make room for your new achievements. Get rid of all the drains on your time and energy – yes, even friends, that take up your time and energy.

Work out your needs, and how to get them met. Needs are different from wants – although psychologists tell us that some wants can come from unsatisfied needs. Do you need love, money, security and motivation? Brainstorm with friends on how to get these needs met.

Ask for more than you need – you'll function better with spare capacity. Compare your energies to your bank account. Don't you feel more confident and energetic when you're well in credit, than when you're fretting about the possibility of being overdrawn on your minimum balance?

Take time for yourself each day – to meditate, relax, dream, visualise.

Lower your expectations – plan, scheme and focus

by all means, but the less you expect in order to make you happy on a daily basis – the happier you'll be.

Work as hard on your relationship as on your goals.

Cut down on negative thinking – read books, take courses, look to experts for help if necessary. You wouldn't seek our toxic foods, or breathe toxic fumes, so why poison your mind with toxic thinking?

APPENDIX A:
BUT WHAT DO THEY
ACTUALLY MEAN?
DEALING WITH THE EXPERTS

Dealing with the experts on your own can be one of the most stressful aspects of heading up your own household. Trying to explain a ping to a car mechanic, or persuade your bank manager not to review your overdraft facility, or emphasise to the builder why you *don't* want a lower lintel is at times enough to make a man weep – and a woman want to give up. Those who have lived to tell the tales of such encounters say that you have to follow the rules:

Know the terminology: if you don't, not only can you misunderstand and be misunderstood, you'll have a harder time earning any respect. Don't try and build up a relationship, or aim to be liked. You're the boss, and paying for your wishes to be carried out. Aim to be pleasant, efficient and courteous, but not pals. Some say that the best, if not the most stressful work is done for fusspots.

Get it in writing: from estimates onwards, and find out what, if any, hidden agendas lurk behind the startlingly low quote. Get phone numbers, names of those in charge and those who can make things happen – they may not be the same.

Keep a diary: dates, times, work periods, deliveries, work done, etc.

Don't rely on given dates: especially if delays may bring debts.

Read a book on assertiveness training before taking on any experts: you need to know how to repeat yourself continually if your flexibility zone has been by-passed, and you are arguing for your basic requirements.

If it all becomes too much, then leave the scene to calm down: tears, rows and hysterics are nothing new to many of the people with whom you may deal, and will weaken your case and argument. In any case, tears as strategy work only for the very young and appealing.

THE BANK MANAGER

Leaving aside all the complaints, resentment and anger – here's what your bank manager would like *you* to know:

He *hates* you to:

✦ go into the red without letting him know in advance. A letter, or phone call would help matters;

✦ bounce cheques/forget to sign them or misdate them;

✦ ignore letters and calls when financial trouble looms;

✦ take on more loans, debts etc. without telling him.

When you go to see your bank manager, be well prepared, with details of assets, loans, re-payments, salary, debts, mortgage. You may never be asked for details, but it could save time wasting. Even if you're positively "invited" to borrow money, you may be asked for full financial details. Explain exactly why you want the loan, how you intend to pay it back, and how long this could take. A mini-business plan or projection, with financial details might help here.

Your bank manager will want to see a good credit risk sitting at his desk. If you can show a regular pattern of savings, prompt re-payments, no missed direct debits, regular in-credit account record, and regular re-payment of any credit card bills, this will all help.

You will be asked about collateral for the loan, and possibly a guarantor as well. Sometimes people don't realise that banks look at the balance, or gearing between your collateral (or fallback means of re-payment) and the means by which you will re-pay the loan. Banks like to see a good balance – which doesn't over-stretch your resources. It has happened that collateral in full, but a meagre salary out of which a loan was to be re-paid wasn't acceptable, and the full amount wasn't lent.

Remember that in many cases, especially in smaller regional branches, your local bank manager will have to send your request to a regional centre, where guidelines can be firm, so the personal recommendation may not count for as much.

LANGUAGE OF THE MONEY MEN

Bear – investor who sells a security in the hope of buying it back later, cheaper.

Bull – investor who buys in the hope of later selling it at a higher price.

Big Four – Barclays, Lloyds, Midland and National Westminster Banks.

Blue Chip – share in one of the largest, safest companies – e.g. ICI, Unilever.

Collateral – assets pledged as security for a loan.

Dividend – pay out to investors in a company. Final – end of year, Interim – half way.

Equity – another term for Ordinary Shares *or* assets, value.

Cum – with.

Ex – without.

Gilt Edged – Government IOUs – British Funds or Government Stock.

Gearing – borrowing – the relationship between borrowed money and equity money.

MLR – Minimum Lending Rate – the lowest interest rate charged to borrowers by the Bank of England. If it goes down, overdrafts are cheaper, and in time so may mortgages and savings rates of return. If it goes up, so does borrowing, and maybe mortgages in time, and savings rates of return.

Liquid Assets – money in cash, or easily converted into cash.

Cash Flow – money generated internally by a company.

Capital Gains Tax – tax payable on profits from sale of most assets, especially shares.

Rights Issue – offer to existing shareholders of further shares.

Scrip Issue – extra shares given out free to existing shareholders.

Rescheduling – rearranging the terms of a loan.

Gross – before tax.

Net – after tax.

Annuity – arrangement by which capital, e.g. a house, is paid into a company scheme in return for a guaranteed income.

Capitalise – to free up capital.

LANGUAGE OF THE MECHANICS

ABS – Anti-Lock Braking
C/L – Central Locking
ESR – Electric Sunroof
E/W – Electric Windows
HRW – Heated Rear Window
LM – Low Mileage
ONO – Or Nearest Offer
PAB – Power Assisted Brakes
RHR – Rear Head Rests
VLM – Very Low Mileage

SYMPTOM	POSSIBLE CAUSES
Starter won't turn, no head-lights	Flat battery, defective starter, electrical failure, seized engine
Engine turns over slowly	Flat battery
Engine won't fire, misfires or pulls back	Ignition, spark plugs, fuel pump, carburettor
Engine 'pinks'	Wrong fuel grade, spark plugs, overheating, ignition timing
Overheating in engine	Coolant, fan belt, cooling fan, water pump, thermo-stat
Excessive noise and/or rattle	Exhaust
Car pulls to one side	Tyre pressure, misalign-ment or tracking, damage to suspension
Oil pressure warning light, plus knocking	Worn crankshaft, oil pres-sure
Brake pedal free, not firm	Air in hydraulics, worn pads/shoes, suspension
Car won't move in gear	Transmission failure
Clutch slips	Worn clutch
Clutch grates, difficult to engage	Adjustment, synchromesh, hydraulic failure
Car pulls to one side when braking	Worn brakes, under inflated tyres

TRANSPORTS OF DELIGHT

New or old, the keys to happy motoring are good advice – from an expert, rather than an enthusiast.

Buying a new car

If you decide to buy a new car:

✦ Check on popularity and resale value.

✦ Check what any warranty entitles you to – and for how long.

✦ Check that the bodywork and trim are as ordered.

✦ Check *all* electricals, as you take delivery.

✦ Report minor faults at once.

✦ With major faults, try first with the dealer, but having kept copies of all correspondence, contact the manufacturer next. Make a fuss.

✦ Take note and discuss the situation over extras you didn't order – or pay for.

✦ Pick a saleable colour – black, dark, metallic, clear primaries, not drab.

✦ Watch trends in body shapes, and keep up with them for re-sale.

✦ Know the mechanical reputation of the model as well as make you have chosen.

Buying a second hand car

Dealers' cars are safer than auctions, although there is still risk, even with expert advice. If you want to try your luck, get a trusted mechanic to go along beforehand – not a male friend who thinks he knows about cars. Arrange to pay the mechanic to check the car –

he may have access to details through contacts, and may even know the reserve price.

The same applies to dealers' second hand cars. Have an expert check it. You, however, should be aware of such factors as your warranty rights – which will inevitably be affected by the age of the car and its mileage. You can't expect an eight-year-old car to work as well as one of just a few months – so allow for some give and take. However, research the dealers' record with customer satisfaction. Look for evidence of use of fillers to cover rust, and uneven bodywork. Check stripes as well, they're sometimes used to hide filler. Ask why the car is being sold, and look for MOT certificates. Check for paintwork mismatch paint oversprays at windows. Look for paint cellulite – may be a sign of rust, and a dirty, dusty engine; all signs of neglect.

If you decide to trade in your existing car as part of the deal, be prepared to shop around and do considerable research:

✦   Is the deal that you are offered on your car *really* a reflection of its market price?

✦   Would you be better to sell it through its own dealer network, or privately advertise? You could save thousands, or perhaps be in a stronger bargaining position.

✦   You need a reasonable warranty period, but check whether it is part of the actual sale price of the car you hope to buy, or, in the case of an extended period, an expensive extra. Just how much of an extended warranty period is economical to you?

✦   Know the weak points of the car you hope to buy, e.g. clutch, rusting, gearbox.

✦   Make a point of asking for details, and establish definitions of reasonable wear and tear.

✦ Watch out for sales techniques, and don't be lulled or pressured into hasty decisions. Don't fall for the "she who hesitates is lost" line, or the regretful downgrading of your existing car – "unusual", "limited market", "older model", "established problems", etc. Remember, if you drive the car, some would say even sit into it, you're half way there to buying, so bide by mother's old rules of "look but don't touch" for those early dates.

✦ Remember, no matter what the salesman says, no model is unique or irreplaceable – a lovely little number, which is even better for your needs will be on that forecourt before you know it.

LANGUAGE OF THE BUILDERS

Header face brick – small end of the brick.
Stretcher face brick – long side of the brick.
Course – name for a single row of bricks.
Pointing – the name for finishing off the joins between bricks or slabs.
Piers – supporting columns for walls.
Riser – the vertical height of a step.
Tread – horizontal part of step, where we walk.
Nosing – the front of the tread.
Coping – protective top, brick or stone, to protect from the elements.
Rendering – finishing for exterior walls, e.g. rough cast or pebbledash.
Lintel – section which rests on bearings to support wall above a door or window.
Cavity wall – wall with inner and outer section of bricks.
Beams – horizontal timbers which support roof.
Rafters – vertical or angled beams which support roof.
Joists – timbers which support ceilings.

Laths – thin wooden battens nailed under joists, and coated with plaster.

Flashing – waterproof join at the junction in a roof, e.g. lead, zinc, aluminium.

Cladding – wall covering, e.g. tiles, slate, brick.

Floating coat – first coat of plaster.

DPC – damp proof course – a plastic ribbon on the base of the wall.

Eaves – lowest part of roof, overhanging supporting wall.

Gable – triangle wall, which meets the ridge of the roof.

LANGUAGE OF THE PLUMBERS

Stack – soil (waste) pipe running from top of house to drains.

Ball valve – controls the flow of water into cold storage tank and WC cistern.

Septic tank – uses bacteria to decompose organic sewage.

Airlock – small amounts of air trapped in part of central heating radiator.

TRV – thermostatic valves.

Hopper head – funnel shaped end of drains, receiving other waste pipes.

Leaking taps – from spout usually means a faulty washer. From beneath head of spout may mean faulty gland pacing. From mixer taps – may mean ring needs to be replaced.

Burst pipes – in emergency, drain off the pipe. Switch off all heaters and boiler. Turn off stopcock. Turn on cold taps, and run out, then hot taps, and immersion heater. Cut a length of hosepipe, slit it, and wrap it over the burst pipe section. Secure it with wire loops, or wire, tied up with pliers to hold in place.

Blocked drains – if from sink, possibly from food remains or grease, try a commercial product (whilst wearing gloves). Or, use a plunger, with water in the sink. If the trap is plastic, and a U bend type, chemicals can be used – with care. If the blockage is in an outdoor gully, possibly caused by leaves, flood debris, etc. wearing heavy gloves, it may be possible to clear it out. If not, try rodding or poking.

Trap – bent section of pipe (U bend or bottle) which holds water to seal out smells.

LANGUAGE OF THE COMPUTER BUFF

CD-ROM – Compact Disc Read Only Memory, a special kind of CD, used in multimedia.

Data – raw material processed by computer systems.

Download – equivalent to office filing away.

DTP – desktop publishing, ideal for those producing newsletters, etc.

DVD – Digital Versatile Disk.

E-mail – electronic mail typed on one computer, and transferred to another instantly.

Encryption – used to ensure security when credit cards are used for purchase on the internet.

Floppy disc – wafers of plastic containing information.

Hard disc drive – a computer's filing space.

Interface – meeting of two computer/information systems with differing characteristics.

Internet – a global computer network.

Internet service providers – companies to which you subscribe that connect you to the internet.

Memory – store for information and data, similar to office desk space.

Menu – comprehensive index of options available, in computer speak.

Modem – device allowing one computer to talk to another over the telephone line.

Mouse – palm sized object, moved on a pad and clicked, to direct computer.

Multimedia – addition of sound and vision to a PC, giving further options.

PC – personal computer.

Screen – where information is displayed, in television monitor style.

Search engine – a means to search and retrieve information on the internet.

Software – components or programmes, for computers.

Surfing the Net – browsing the Internet an computers.

Telecommuting – office work done at home on your computer.

Teleconferencing – meeting or conference of people connected by telecommunications links

WWW – World Wide Web – user friendly subset of the Internet.

Yahoo – directory collection on the Internet.

APPENDIX B:
50 THINGS TO DO IN THIS
LIFETIME (AT LEAST ONCE)

1. Send flowers to a loved one of any age or either sex.
2. Fly on Concorde – try one of the special short trips advertised.
3. Have an affair with someone you adore and fancy – no matter how unsuitable.
4. Stay at a top hotel for a weekend – the Ritz in London or Paris, for example.
5. Go up in a balloon at dawn or sunset.
6. Drive a top of the range sports car.
7. Plant a tree in your name.
8. Run in a marathon.
9. Learn to sing or dance.
10. Arrange to be served breakfast in bed – with all the trimmings.
11. Own a designer dress.
12. Have a bubble bath, with scented candles, and sip a glass of champagne.
13. Learn about wine.
14. Learn to speak another language really well.
15. Throw someone a surprise party.
16. Attend a society ball.
17. Get published – in a local magazine, or newspaper.
18. Surf the Net.
19. Bid at an auction.
20. Learn basic DIY skills – know how to paint a wall, put up brackets and change a wheel.
21. Drink hot chocolate and cinnamon in the winter snow.
22. Sample chocolate from the top chocolatiers in the world.

23. Sleep in a four poster bed.
24. Wear silk underwear.
25. Fly in a helicopter.
26. Write a love letter, on beautiful paper, and seal the envelope with wax.
27. Go for a photography session.
28. Work out the family tree, have it drawn, framed and hung.
29. Frame all those pictures of your loved ones, and display them.
30. Walk barefoot in the sand on a perfect beach.
31. Learn to mix cocktails.
32. Bake your own bread.
33. Teach yourself how to arrange flowers skilfully.
34. Go on stage – even if it's just for a local charity.
35. Write a book – a local guidebook, or on your special interest or hobby.
36. Make a mark – sponsor, donate or auction something for a cause you believe in.
37. Start saving up some mad money – and blow it, on a weekend away, or on fun.
38. Learn to paint or draw.
39. Have a sketch or painting of yourself done – go to your local art school or centre.
40. Have a makeover.
41. Go on holiday at the last minute – try potluck with a cancellation booking.
42. Learn to dance Scottish reels.
43. Get up and join a group to hear the summer dawn chorus.
44. See a summer or winter sunrise or sunset over a megalithic monument.
45. Wear a hat that suits you.
46. Wear period costume for a fancy dress party or ball.
47. Keep a diary.
48. Create one dish, which you can cook superbly and easily from memory.
49. Attend a star studded film premiere.

50. Put something back into your community –
    teach someone to read or write.

APPENDIX C:
RESOURCE LIBRARY
REPUBLIC OF IRELAND

The following is a selection of the Family, Marital, Health and Counselling services that are available. For further details, contact your local library, council or service directory and guides to evening clases.

Counselling and Health

AWARE (Depression support), Tel. 01 6766166

Family Therapy and Counselling Centre, 46 Elmwood Road, Dublin 6, Tel. 01 497 1188

Irish Assoc. for Counselling and Therapy, 8 Cumberland Street, Dun Laoghaire, Tel. 01 230 0061

Irish Assoc. of Holistic Medicine, 66 Eccles Street, Dublin 1, Tel. 01 830 7191

Institute of Psychosynthesis, 19 Clyde Road, Dublin 4, Tel. 01 668 4687

Marriage and Relationship Counselling Services, 24 Grafton Street, Dublin 2, Tel. 01 679 9341

Mental Health Assoc. of Ireland, 6 Adelaide Street, Dun Laoghaire, Tel. 01 284 1166

Psychological Society of Ireland, 2a Corn Exchange Place, Dublin 2, Tel. 01 671 7122

Recovery Inc, Cherry Orchard Hospital, Dublin 10, Tel. 01 626 0775

Turning Point, 23 Crofton Road, Dun Laoghaire, Tel. 01 280 7888

Educational courses, groups and associations

Association for Adventure Sports, Hse of Sport, Long Mile Road, Dublin 12, Tel. 01 450 9845

Ballymaloe Cookery School, Shanagarry, Midleton, Co. Cork, Tel. 021 646 785

Betty Ann Norton Theatre School, Clonbrock House, 11 Harcourt Street, Dublin 2, Tel. 01 4751913

Conservation Volunteers, Ireland, The Green, Griffith College, South Circular Road, Dublin 8, Tel. 01 454 7185

Dingle Writing Courses Ltd, Ballintlea, Ventry, Co. Kerry, Tel. 066 915 9052

Gaiety School of Acting, Sycamore Street, Temple Bar, Dublin 2, Tel. 01 679 9277

The Paint Box, Tel. 091 569579

Trinity Arts Workshop, 191 Pearse Street Dublin 2 Tel. 01 608 2725. Write to P.O. Box 26, Regent House, Trinity College, Dublin 3, Tel. 01 475 1913

Walton's New School of Music, 69 S. Gt. George's Street, Dublin 2, Tel. 01 478 1884

Women's Groups and Associations

Consult Current IPA Yearbook in local library

Work

Country Enterprise Boards – see locations

Dublin City Enterprise Board, 17 Eustace Street, Temple Bar, Dublin 2, Tel.01 677 6068

Enterprise Link, Tel. 1850 35 3333 Telework Ireland, 7 Clones Road, Co. Monaghan

FAS, Baggot Street, Dublin 4, Tel. 01 607 0500

Irish Management Institute, Clonard, Sandyford, Dublin 16, Tel. 01 295 6911

THE IMPOSSIBLE
TAKES LONGER

BIBLIOGRAPHY

Chase, L. (1998) Money – *How to Make More of it*, (Orion Business Books, London)

Cunningham, M. (1998) *Investment Advice for Life*, (Bank of Ireland Asset Management Team, London)

Dowling, C. (1998) *The Myth of the Money Tree*, (Harper Collins, London)

Dublin Enterprise Support Directory, (Dublin Enterprise Forum)

Halson, P. (1999) *Happily Ever After*, (Pan Books, London)

Herman, L. (2000) *Managing your Image in a Week*, (Hodder & Stoughton for the Institute of Management, London).

Levene, T. *The Express – The Woman's Guide to Finance*, (Kogan Page, London)

Llyod Platt, V. (2000) *Secrets of Relationship Success*, (Vermilion, London)

Mullally, M. (1998) *Law and the Family in Ireland*, (Blackhall Publishing, Dublin)

Mullally, M. (1999) *Law and the Family in the UK*, (Blackhall Publishing, Dublin)

Persaud, R. (1997) *Staying Sane*, (Metro Books, London)

Wilde, S. (1998) *The Money Bible*, (Rider, an imprint of Ebury Press, London)

Journal articles

Holmes, T. H. & Rahe, R. H., The Social Re-adjustments Rating Scale, *Journal of Psychosomatic Research* (1967) V11. pp 213-18.

Nowhere else makes you feel this good.

Champneys is set in 170 acres of delightful parkland estate, high in the Chiltern Hills, located only one hour from central London and only 45 minutes from Heathrow or Luton airports.

The perfect place to restore mind, body and soul with an unrivalled range of over 100 treatments and therapies from which to choose, including many medical services and alternative therapies. Our approach to health, beauty and well being is individual, stimulating and rewarding and above all ensures that 'Nowhere else makes you feel this good'.

We would like to offer readers a 10% reduction, on our standard tariff, for stays of 2 nights or more. For reservations please contact us on 01442 291111 quoting "BO1" All stays are subject to availability and cannot be combined with any other offer.

CHAMPNEYS
MIND · BODY · SOUL

Nowhere else makes you feel this good.

Wigginton, Tring, Hertfordshire, HP23 6HY.
Telephone: +44 (0)1442 291111 Facsimile: +44 (0)1442 291112
E-mail: reservations@champneys.co.uk Website: www.champneys.com

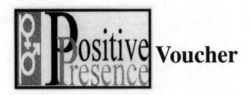 **Voucher**

Value £15.00
to be used towards

Image Consultation

- asesses objectively your overall image
- appraises *your* existing wardrobe
- audits your individual Image Ingredients: voice, non-verbal and grooming
- addresses *Smart Casual Confusion Syndrom* if relevant
- prioritises recommendations to provide maximum impact

18a Lambolle Place, London, Tel 020 7586 7925
Fax 020 7586 7926

Nearest Underground: Belsize Park (Northern) Swiss Cottage (Jubilee)